History of Mexico

A Captivating Guide to Mexican History, Starting from the Rise of Tenochtitlan through Maximilian's Empire to the Mexican Revolution and the Zapatista Indigenous Uprising

Free Bonus from Captivating History
(Available for a Limited time)

Hi History Lovers!

Now you have a chance to join our exclusive history list so you can get your first history ebook for free as well as discounts and a potential to get more history books for free! Simply visit the link below to join.

Captivatinghistory.com/ebook

Also, make sure to follow us on Facebook, Twitter and Youtube by searching for Captivating History.

Contents

INTRODUCTION 1

CHAPTER 1 – THE ERA OF EMPIRES 3

CHAPTER 2 – THE SPANISH-AZTEC WAR AND NEW SPAIN 12

CHAPTER 3 – THE BIRTH OF A NATION 23

CHAPTER 4 – "FROM THE HALLS OF MONTEZUMA..."..........30

CHAPTER 5 – THE BIG DIVISION 40

CHAPTER 6 – "THE MOST BEAUTIFUL EMPIRE IN THE WORLD".......45

CHAPTER 7 – IN THE TIMES OF DON PORFIRIO 54

CHAPTER 8 – THE MEXICAN REVOLUTION.............................61

CHAPTER 9 – THE CRISTEROS 70

CHAPTER 10 – THE SECOND WORLD WAR AND THE MEXICAN MIRACLE 75

CHAPTER 11 – END OF CENTURY PANGS....................................82

CONCLUSION: MEXICO 90

BIBLIOGRAPHY...94

Introduction

Mexico is one of the most distinguishable shapes from space. The country's flag, of green, white, and red fields, contains the image of an eagle with spread wings standing on a cactus. Like few flags in the world, which mostly have celestial objects or colors representing ideals, Mexico's flag has terrestrial imagery, two animals—an eagle and a snake—and a historic moment: the moment when a group of emigrants called the Mexica arrived in the Valley of Mexico. The basin was full of interconnected lakes and snow-capped volcanoes, and it was where the newcomers saw a great bird in the center of the largest body of water. The city of Tenochtitlan, modern-day Mexico City, was founded on that site.

Other flags of the world have animals, mostly birds, as is the case of Mexico's, which traditionally represent freedom, might, or contact with the heavens. But certainly, no other flag has a snake, which is typically a representation of evil. For Mexicans, who are educated since childhood in its meaning, the symbol of the Mexican flag sums up the eternal and historic struggle between two forces, a destructive one, which seems to be intimately woven into the country's character, and a liberating and magnanimous one.

Like most flags of the world, Mexico's insignia speaks of its mythical origins. The image of the eagle on the cactus and the prickly pears, besides being an important moment in the history of the land and a motif that whispers deeply to the psyche of every Mexican, is also a reminder that before an independent country called Mexico existed, there were great cities in its valleys, jungles, and on its lakes—yes, *on* its lakes—which formed empires. Original civilizations arose in very few places on the planet without learning from other cultures, and as such, these people living in isolation from other societies created numerical systems, a writing system, and their own lifestyle in an autonomous and different way. Mexico was one of those places. Before the modern country was born in 1821, the territory that today comprises 32 states and few small islands was inhabited by ancient dynasties and kingdoms of warriors, astronomers, priests, temples for human sacrifice, and, surprisingly, some of the largest cities in the world. It is estimated that the sacred city of Chichen Itza, in the Yucatan Peninsula, was larger than Paris at its height of splendor. This fascinating journey through Mexico's history, from its amazing pre-Hispanic past to the end of the 20th century, will reveal more surprises than the reader can imagine. In the words of the self-proclaimed Mexican singer Chavela Vargas, "Mexico has magic. I looked for that magic, and I found it there."

Chapter 1 – The Era of Empires

Long before the emergence of empires in ancient Mexico, the first humans arrived from the north, descending along the western coast of North America or sailing along the seashore southward approximately thirteen thousand years ago. The first settlers surely arrived in intermittent small bands and settled mostly in the region now known as Mesoamerica, in southern Mexico and Central America. Approximately seven thousand years ago, the first seeds were harvested.

The first great civilization in the American continent arose in Mexico at the same time as the Babylonians in Asia, the so-called Olmecs, in what are now the southern states of Mexico. The Olmecs had their own writing system and calendar. Little is known, however, of Mexico's first great culture, including what name they gave themselves. The word Olmec is of a later origin and means "inhabitant of the rubber country." The area of Mexico where they flourished—the states of Veracruz and Tabasco—is extremely humid and dissolved the human remains of these ancient inhabitants, so it remains unknown what they looked like. Famously, this civilization left, among other things, the gigantic Olmec heads that, for centuries, were hidden in the jungle until they were discovered in the mid-19th century. The physical features of these heads, which presumably represent the Olmecs, continues to attract the attention of anthropologists for their obvious African features, with their round head, oblique eyes, short and wide nose, and thick lips. The proposal that the Olmecs were migrants from sub-Saharan Africa, or that at least the culture had contact with ancient sailors from the so-called Dark Continent, although fanciful, has not been completely dismissed. The Olmecs, who erected several cities, eventually scattered in the jungle around 100 BCE and eventually assimilated into other groups.

Two Empires

With the change of the era, at a time when Christianity was spreading in the Middle East and Turkey, the first cities flourished in the center of Mexico, along with other aspects that accompany the birth of a civilization: a political system, hieroglyphic writing, palaces, markets, a bureaucracy, and armies.

The city of Teotihuacan, a word that means "the place where the gods dwell," was the first metropolis in North America, founded in 300 BCE. Its impressive pyramids are preserved today in the vicinity of Mexico City. According to a legend that the later Aztecs preserved, the gods gathered in Teotihuacan to create the moon, the sun, and the other celestial bodies. At its time of splendor, the city had more than one hundred thousand inhabitants, which was a smaller population but still similar to great cities like Alexandria, Ephesus, Carthage, and Antioch, making it one of the ten most populated cities in the world at the time. But certainly in those other cities of Asia and Africa, which at the moment were buoyant centers of Christianity, people would have been horrified to see the public rituals that were carried out in the form of human sacrifices and other ceremonies for the gods at the top of the great pyramids of the sun and the moon. These rites continued for many centuries.

Teotihuacan dominated central Mexico without rivals. The priests, warriors, merchants, and artisans were the basis of its power. All houses had drainage systems and a central courtyard. Its inhabitants lived in that place until the 9th century CE. The culture of Teotihuacan was transmitted with such impetus to later civilizations that even centuries after the metropolis was abandoned, the inhabitants of ancient Mexico still made pilgrimages to seek the favor of gods like Tlaloc (the god of water) and especially Quetzalcoatl, the god of wind and air (similar to how Yahweh was for the ancient Hebrews, a storm god). Quetzalcoatl was represented by a feathered serpent. This god, whose first record of worship comes from the 1st century CE in Teotihuacan, eventually acquired messianic characteristics, and the Spanish conquerors associated it with the figure of Jesus Christ or with Thomas the Apostle.

Quetzalcoatl, the god of the wind, the morning star (Venus), the deity who stole corn to give it to men, the entity that sprayed the bones in the realm of the dead with blood in order to give life to humans, was also a person with a story, possibly a historical character that became merged with the god. His name was Ce-acatl Topiltizin, and he was a priest who had been conceived miraculously when his mother swallowed a precious stone. A virtuous and beloved man, he taught people the secrets of life and heaven and was deceived by an antagonistic witch who got him drunk and killed his followers. Quetzalcoatl fled and disappeared into the sea, where he promised that one day he would return to claim his own. Spanish sources fed by Native American informants refer to him as a divine man who wore a white robe and banned human sacrifice. Not surprisingly, the Spanish priests thought that the Mexica (the so-called "Aztecs" by later scholars) were talking about an apostle or perhaps Jesus himself. In fact, although it is not an official doctrine of the Mormons, some sectors of this church have tried to associate, even to this date, the figure of this ancient priest with that of the historical Jesus.

It is not so clear, however, as it was previously believed, if the Aztecs or Mexica were waiting for the return of Quetzalcoatl when the Spanish conquerors made their arrival and if the city gates were opened to the invaders because the Native Americans thought the

Spaniards were Quetzalcoatl's appointed. The version that Montezuma stepped aside and handed over his throne to Hernán Cortés when he saw him is most likely a fictional story created by Cortés in order to justify his actions. Today, prominent historians concede that these two myths—the Spaniards as gods, and the submissive surrender of Montezuma—are an invention of the conquerors *after the city's fall.* Just a few years after the destruction of Tenochtitlan, there was already evidence of the myth of Cortés as Quetzalcoatl. Anthropologists have found images of Quetzalcoatl in almost all of Mexico's current territory, from Sinaloa in the northwest to the south, which shows that at the time of the meeting of the two cultures, its mythology was already disseminated throughout the region.

Around the same time as Teotihuacan dominated the central plateau, the Mayas flourished on the Yucatan Peninsula, and they were perhaps the earliest advanced civilization on the American continent. From the 19th century onward, their history, ceremonial centers, cyclical calendar, mathematics, and writings generated fascination among anthropologists. The Mayas were captivated with the universe, including its time and measures. In their observatories, they calculated the duration of the year and the motion of Venus. They also discovered the existence of planets moving over the background of motionless stars, invented constellations, recorded eclipses, and established the existence of great cosmic cycles to measure the passage of time, from one year to a 400-year cycle until reaching the major time span, the so-called "Alautun," whose duration was millions of years. The exact duration of their eras is not known since there are currently discrepancies in the interpretation.

At first, it was believed that the Maya of Yucatan had formed a harmonious empire dedicated to mathematics, observing the stars, and building impressive monuments that survive to this day, but this idea has now been abandoned, especially after the discovery of the murals of Bonampak, the most extensive conserved of that culture.

Now we know that the Mayan kingdoms lived in a state of permanent warfare with each other. The city of Chichen Itza, the last great Mayan city to emerge in the jungle, left an impressive pyramid of 365 steps, one for each day of the year, the largest ballgame in the Americas, an astronomical observatory, and skull altars.

In southern Mexico, Monte Albán (in the modern state of Oaxaca), founded on top of a mountain, came to dominate a huge area and had artisans in Teotihuacan. Its residents worshiped more than forty gods. At the beginning of the 6th century, two great cultures, the Maya and Teotihuacan, coexisted on both extremes of the land and established commercial relations, thus extending their influence, their language, their gods, and their architecture to the entire central region of the country we now call Mexico.

The First Mexico

"At the edge of the cave they saw an erect eagle on the cactus devouring happily, tearing things apart when eating, and so [when] the eagle saw them, it ducked very much its head."

—*Mexicayotl Chronicle*, 16th century

But the most representative civilization of ancient Mexico, in fact the most important and authentic expression of "empire" on the American continent, was the Mexica or Aztec civilization, whose importance was so great that its symbols, name, and even culture persist in the country. The leaders of modern Mexico have dug through the history and culture of the Aztecs in search of motifs for the creation of a national identity. The word "Aztec," though, is of modern origin. The inhabitants of ancient Mexico would have preferred to call themselves "Mexica," and they were a part of a larger group called the Nahua, whose language was Nahuatl, the lingua franca of the time. Many words in Nahuatl survive in the Spanish spoken in Mexico today. For example, the Spanish language assimilated words like "cocoa," "chili," "coyote," "tomato," "guacamole," and "chocolate," among many others. When the Aztec Empire arose in central Mexico, not far from the place where the great city of Teotihuacan and its pyramids once stood, the great civilizations of the classical period had already dissolved. Teotihuacan had been abandoned, with the reasons for its sudden disappearance still unclear. In Yucatan, the populous Mayan cities had been swallowed by the jungle.

The Mexica, a migrant group from northern Mexico, reached what is now Mexico City around 1325 CE, following the prophecy of one of their gods. On their pilgrimage, they stopped in the sacred and abandoned city of Teotihuacan to ask for divine guidance. Their arrival in the Valley of Mexico was not easy. They were attacked by the peoples already established there, who expelled them from their countries. Exhausted, and without resources, the Mexica were surrounded by hostile cities and confined to inhospitable places. Persecuted to the shore of the great lake of Texcoco, the Mexica built rafts and entered the waters to save their lives. There, they hid among the reeds, islets, and swampy lands, among the aquatic vegetation of Texcoco, where they remade their forces and fled once again. Across the lake, going from side to side, according to the story that Dominican Friar Diego Durán collected years later, they saw the sign that their god Huitzilopochtli had given them so that they would know the place where they should settle, their promised land or, more exactly, their promised *water*—an eagle on top of a cactus. Thus, the people that had roamed for so long ended its exodus of more than two hundred years with the installation of the first stone of their temple on the lake. This narrative, the "official" story that the Aztecs told the Europeans, might be idealized. When the Mexica passed from a small subdued human group to the greatest empire of pre-Hispanic Mexico, they burned the previous accounts and wrote a new history where they were the ones chosen to rule the world.

What is indisputable is that over time, the humble aquatic settlement became one of the largest cities in the world. There, they built their capital on an islet in the middle of a lake. It seems that the piece of land where the Aztecs built their very first village was called

"Mexico," meaning "in the center of the moon lake." The whole city was named Tenochtitlan. Those insignificant islets and their surroundings were spaces with abundant fishing, hunting, and gathering, meaning it was an ideal place to settle. Their position in the middle of a lake also gave them a strategic advantage: avoiding friction with neighboring cities, which were involved in unceasing expansionist wars. The lack of defined physical boundaries facilitated neutrality and concrete agreements and alliances. Thus, an insignificant hamlet became a metropolis in a few decades.

At this time, there emerged a philosophy of war that was closely linked to the cosmos, the idea that continuous human sacrifices were necessary to help the sun in its daily struggle against the forces of darkness and to sustain the battle of the eagle and tiger knights on behalf of the uninterrupted movement of stars and planets. In the archaeological record, representations of human sacrifices began to multiply at this time. But not everything was barbarism and cruelty. At the same time, the arts and education flourished; the Aztec, or Mexica, created sculptures, paintings, and other works; in the apogee of the Aztec Empire, more than sixty thousand canoes converged every day in the city of Tenochtitlan, which was supported on piles and trunks in the style of Venice and was larger than any European capital of the 15th century.

The inhabitants of Tenochtitlan planted crops on firm land and also on floating islands called *chinampas*, which were supported with piles. There were up to a thousand people in charge of cleaning the streets, which were swept every day, and the garbage was incinerated in huge fires that brightened the streets at night. Since Texcoco was a salty lake, there were also canals or aqueducts that carried water from nearby springs for a population that, it is worth mentioning, was neat and clean as in modern standards, and who enjoyed taking a daily bath.

Their economic, political, and social organization reached a very high level. In the nearby Tlatelolco market—which still persists in some form today—up to fifty thousand people gathered on market days. In Tlatelolco, people bought and sold with the local currency (cocoa beans), and the city was adorned by temples, palaces, and statues in the streets, squares, and other important points. When the first Europeans saw Tenochtitlan, a city greater than any of those in Europe, suddenly appearing in the misty valley, floating on a lake surrounded by snowy volcanoes, they wondered if they were seeing visions. An advanced civilization that had flourished independently of the Old World was in front of their very eyes.

One of those first witnesses, the Spaniard Hernán Cortés, left a valuable description of the great city, a kind of American Venice divided in four quarters separated by four avenues that radiated from the center and crossed by canals where people traveled in canoes that went from one place to another. Cortés wrote:

This great city of Temixtitan [sic] is situated in this salt lake, and from the main land to the denser parts of it, by whichever route one chooses to enter, the distance is two leagues. There are four avenues or entrances to the city, all of which are formed by artificial causeways, two spears' length in width. The city is as large as Seville or Cordoba; its streets, I speak of the principal ones, are very wide and straight; some of these, and all the inferior ones, are half land and half water, and are navigated by canoes. All the streets at intervals have openings, through which the water flows, crossing from one street to another; and at these openings, some of which are very wide, there are also very wide bridges, composed of large pieces of timber, of great strength and well put together; on many of these bridges ten horses can go abreast.

Cortés and his companions were amazed at the commercial activity that took place in Tenochtitlan and the neighboring Tlatelolco. Cortés wrote in his letters, or "relations," to Spain that the city had many public squares, where markets and other places for buying and selling items were situated. A particular square, according to the conqueror, was twice the size of Salamanca (located in Spain) and completely surrounded by porticoes, where every day, more than sixty thousand people gathered to trade—a city in itself. "All kinds of merchandise that the world affords [are found], embracing the necessaries of life, as for instance articles of food, as well as jewels of gold and silver, lead, brass, copper, tin, precious stones, bones, shells, snails, and feathers."

The city had an herb street, where people bought an infinite variety of roots and medicinal herbs (which, to this day, Mexicans are still very fond of). There were barbershops where people cut their hair or went just to wash it, as well as many stores where food and drinks were consumed—in other words, the predecessors of modern restaurants. "The way of living among the people," Cortés wrote, incredulous that such a civilization could exist outside the Christian world, "is very similar to that of Spain, and considering that this is a barbarian nation, separated from the knowledge of the true God or the communication with enlightened nations, one may well marvel at the order and good governance that is maintained wherever it may be."

This was the city of Mexico in the first decades of the 16th century. But a traumatic event, which would forever transform the face of the region and the entire continent, would cause the Aztecs to lose everything in an ear-splitting collapse. Their city, their culture, their families, and their own nation would suddenly come to an end. That curse came floating by the sea on Good Friday, April 22nd, 1519.

Chapter 2 – The Spanish-Aztec War and New Spain

"The invaders saw things never seen or ever dreamed of."

—*Mexicayotl Chronicle*

"When we gazed upon all this splendour at once, we scarcely knew what to think, and we doubted whether all that we beheld was real. A series of large towns stretched themselves along the banks of the lake, out of which still larger ones rose magnificently above the waters. Innumerable crowds of canoes were plying everywhere around us; at regular distances we continually passed over new bridges, and before us lay the great city of Mexico in all its splendour."

—Bernal Díaz

In 1519, while an expedition commanded by Hernán Cortés touched the Yucatan Peninsula, 1,300 kilometers (almost 808 miles) away, in what is now the historic center of Mexico City, Emperor Montezuma II, the ninth king of the Aztecs, ruled a vast territory that comprised the entire southern half of Mexico. These lands were brimming with peoples subjected to the Aztecs and who were resentful of the intolerable tributes, including humans necessary for the sacrifices to placate the gods. From the steps of the main temple of Tenochtitlan, the blood of those sacrificed to the gods descended like rivers.

The Aztecs believed that once a victim was sacrificed, their blood was carried by eagles, allowing the cosmos to maintain its order and the sun to rise every morning. The myths of salvation were adapted to military interests: those who died in war went to the sky of the sun led by Teoyaomiqui, a goddess who wore a necklace made of hearts, hands, and skulls, and whose head was Death itself. Sometimes Teoyaomiqui was represented as being decapitated, and from her neck sprouted streams of blood in the form of snakes. The bodies of women who died in their first birth became sacred, and the young soldiers tried to steal parts of them, especially the hair and fingers, to make talismans that hung from their shields. The children who died at the age of breastfeeding went to a place where there was a tree whose branches dripped milk, those who died from causes related to water went to a place where everything existed in abundance, and those who died a natural death were not rewarded or punished because they had simply fulfilled their destiny.

Some scholars have estimated that the Aztecs sacrificed more than two hundred thousand people per year, and on the days of the re-consecration of the great pyramid of Tenochtitlan, there was an average of fifteen human sacrifices per minute. It was from that splendid and bloody center of the Aztec Empire that Montezuma extended trade routes to Panama. Several indigenous peoples—the Tlaxcalans, the Huastecos, the Totonacs, and many more, who produced an abundance of corn, cocoa, vanilla, fruits, cotton, and precious woods—received visits from tax collectors and paid tributes that were hateful to them. Although they occasionally rebelled, fed up with the Aztec domain, they were firmly subdued by the Triple Alliance, which had Tenochtitlan at its head. The Mayan peoples, who were past their time of splendor, were too far away and not organized but fragmented in many small kingdoms throughout the Yucatan Peninsula. During his reign, Montezuma also raised the demands in the education of the youth, but like all Aztec emperors, who were faithful servants of the god of war, Huitzilopochtli, Montezuma sat on his throne under a kind of black cloud, a kind of fatalism about an uncertain future envisioned by the astrologers of his court.

The Meeting

Montezuma was 45 when a Spanish vessel shipwrecked on its way from Panama to the island of Santo Domingo, located in the Antilles Sea. It was the year 1511. The sailors drifted for several days until they saw some unknown beaches, which, at first, they thought was yet another island. Without knowing it, they would become the first Spaniards to put their foot on the American mainland, a continent hitherto unknown to European navigators. When they entered what is now Yucatan in search of supplies, they were attacked by the Mayas. Although almost all of them died, at least two managed to save their lives, a sailor named Jerónimo de Aguilar and another named Gonzalo Guerrero. Two years later, Hernán Cortés arrived on the island of Cozumel, where he heard that a couple of Spanish shipwrecks lived there, and he went to rescue them.

When he found his fellow countryman Jerónimo de Aguilar, he did not recognize him; after eight years, he had lost his fluency in Spanish, he was dressed as a Mayan, and his skin was brown. But Aguilar knew the language of the Yucatec people, and Cortés knew that was going to be of great advantage to him, and indeed, he later employed Aguilar as an interpreter.

Aguilar recognized the Spanish ships and went to look for his shipwrecked companion Gonzalo Guerrero, who lived in another village. But his comrade of adversity refused to go with the expedition. His words were kept in the annals of the soldier and chronicler Bernal Díaz: "Brother, I am married and have three kids. Go with God, that I have my face carved and my eyebrows pierced [in the Mayan style]. And you see these my little children, how beautiful they are!" Guerrero was so esteemed in his town that he had been designated captain in times of war. He was also, namely, the father of the first modern Mexican, that is, the offspring of a European man and a Native American woman. Aguilar tried to talk his partner into joining the expedition, telling him that if he so desired, he could take his children with him. Guerrero's wife, a Mayan woman, rebuked Aguilar and asked him to leave. Nothing could change Guerrero's mind, who lived among the Mayas until the end of his life. He died, ironically, fighting against the Spaniards.

The next decisive meeting of Cortés occurred days later when, in March of 1519, he arrived at the modern state of Tabasco, on the coast of the Gulf of Mexico, on his way south. There, he received from a native lord a group of twenty young female slaves that Cortés distributed among his men. A remarkable woman of about nineteen to twenty years old was in that group—her birthdate can only be approximated. She was called Malinalli. Malinalli had a sad story to tell. Her father had married for the second time and sold her as a slave to some merchants, who, in turn, handed her over to a chief in Tabasco who met Cortés on his way to Tenochtitlan. Jerónimo de Aguilar, the castaway rescued in Yucatan, noted that young Malinalli, who according to oral tradition was beautiful and cultured, spoke the Mayan language and another tongue he couldn´t understand, which was Nahuatl. Since Malinalli could communicate with Aguilar, an efficient combination of interpreters was thus formed: Cortés spoke in Spanish with Aguilar, Aguilar spoke in Mayan with Malinalli, and then she translated the message in Nahuatl for the Native Americans. In this way, Cortés was able to communicate with Emperor Montezuma. In command of 518 soldiers, 110 sailors, 16 horse riders, 32 crossbowmen, 13 gunmen, ten cannons, and four falconets, Cortés took the young woman for himself and made her his faithful companion, lover, and confidant. Devoted and supportive, Malinalli was at his side through all of the hazards and decisive moments of the conquest of the Aztec Empire. The young woman called Malinalli, who was baptized as Marina by the Spaniards and later known as Malinche by the Mexicans, is to date, due to her proximity to the invaders, one of the most controversial women in the history of Mexico. There is even a word derived from her name to refer to excessive love for all things foreign and the betrayal of one's own: Malinchism.

A month after these events, on April 21st, 1519, Cortés and his eleven ships touched the coast of Veracruz. There, Cortés founded the first city in continental America: Villa Rica de la Veracruz, one of the most important ports today. Along the way, two unexpected developments happened that encouraged the expedition to move inland: the chiefs and *caciques* (minor local bosses) that Cortés was finding were offering him alliances since they wanted to free themselves from Montezuma, and they provided him with valuable information on what he would find inland. The other surprise was the arrival of the first ambassadors of Montezuma, who had traveled to the Gulf of Mexico to meet Cortés; they had gifts, which consisted of much gold, and encouraged him to turn around and leave. The strategy had the opposite effect, as they only aroused Cortés's interest and the greed of his men. When the Spanish expedition finally went up and down the mountains and saw the city on the lake in the distance, it was the month of November 1519. They gazed in awe at the pyramids, water canals, which were full of canoes, gardens, and thousands of men, women, and children. They were speechless, "gazing on such wonderful sights, we did not know what to say, or whether what appeared before us was real," wrote Bernal Díaz years later, remembering everything he had seen and heard.

When Cortés entered Tenochtitlan and met the monarch, the king of the largest city on the continent, both men bowed deeply to each other or exchanged necklaces, or Cortés tried to hold him in the European style, and then two lords stopped him from touching Montezuma. The accounts vary. Nonetheless, the meeting was friendly but tense. Both sides displayed their diplomatic skills, but the clash of cultures was imminent. For the moment, both men could communicate with each other thanks to Malinalli, the young indigenous woman who had stood by Cortés's side since Tabasco and understood the emperor's language. Malinalli was probably the most astonished of all, being in front of that powerful lord she had only heard rumors of.

Montezuma took Cortés to some spacious rooms and then returned with gold, silver, feathers, and other gifts. It was an important moment not only in the history of Mexico but of humanity: the meeting between Montezuma and Hernán Cortés in the place where Mexico City stands today symbolizes the moment when humanity and civilization, which, in the beginning, moved east and west from the Fertile Crescent, came full circle and found itself again. It was one of the most important meetings of human history. That day, the earth became a global village. The idea that the natives saw the Spaniards as gods and that they knelt before them, or that they saw Quetzalcoatl in Cortés, are later developments, a part of the victors' propaganda and excuses of the defeated. There is no evidence in Aztec history prior to this encounter that Montezuma was really waiting for the return of the god. On the contrary, the encounter seems to have been between two equally proud and confident forces. And it is even possible that Emperor Montezuma was actually in full control of the situation, planning to put his newest acquisitions in cages or ritually sacrifice them.

For months, life between visitors and locals was cordial, but things were boiling beneath the surface. Cortés, suspicious all the time, feared for his safety, and finally, fearing a betrayal, he arrested Montezuma. Since the search for allies was one of the routine procedures of the Spaniards in conquest wars, Cortés took advantage of the hostility of the many people who were against the Aztecs and formed alliances to conquer Tenochtitlan. Several indigenous kingdoms shared his purpose: to see Montezuma's fall. It was not, as has been said many times before, a handful of brave Spanish adventurers or Cortés's genius that conquered the vast empire; rather, it was a situation more similar to a civil war or, more precisely, a rebellion of all the subjugated peoples against the Triple Alliance. The Aztec Empire was, in many ways, conquered by other Native Americans.

The hostilities began when Cortés was absent from the city for a few days. One of his captains committed a massacre against the civilian population that was celebrating in the Templo Mayor. The furious Mexica rebelled en masse. The most widespread version is that Emperor Montezuma died during this episode when Cortés returned to Tenochtitlan and asked him to go out and talk to his countrymen, appealing them to retreat. But his bellicose citizens supposedly stoned him. However, both this incident, as with others related to the conquest of Mexico, should be taken with a grain of salt as possible inventions of Europeans to blame the incident on the Aztec people and not on the Spaniards. The Montezuma Codex, which is preserved in the National Library of Anthropology and History of Mexico, is a fragmentary amate codex of the 16th century that contains people and historical scenes with texts written in Nahuatl in Latin characters. There is a drawing of Montezuma with a rope tied to his neck held by a Spaniard. Beside this scene is a stabbed Native American. Above one can see the Templo Mayor of Tenochtitlan burning in flames. At the top is Cortés on horseback. The codex shows, it seems, the major events of the siege of Tenochtitlan, including the destruction of the city and the killing of Montezuma by the Spaniards.

After the massacre at the Templo Mayor, Cortés and his men suffered a devastating defeat and were expelled from Tenochtitlan. They were almost annihilated. At this point, history could have changed, but the Aztecs inexplicably did not follow them to exterminate them. Once he was free from harm, Cortés, shattered, sat down to cry under a tree, an incident known as "The Tragic Night." The tree where Cortés shed bitter tears still exists in Mexico City, although it is very deteriorated after an intentional fire in 1980. The

Aztecs lost their chance to liquidate the invaders due to the arrival of a new and much more ruthless enemy: smallpox.

With the help of nearly 200,000 Native American allies, peoples who were conquered by the Aztecs, Cortés regained his strength and put Tenochtitlan under siege. Like all historic sieges, this one was prolonged and cruel. Cortés cut off the water supply, and virtually all the peoples of the region, who had been oppressed for over a hundred years and forced to contribute their share of men and women for human sacrifice, supported the Europeans, meaning no one was coming to Tenochtitlan's aid. When Tenochtitlan fell, more than forty thousand bodies were floating on Lake Texcoco. The enemies of the Aztecs showed no mercy, and the events that took place after the city's fall practically amounted to genocide. Within a couple of years of Cortés's arrival, and without going through a phase of decline like other empires, the most powerful ruler that had existed in Mexico was dead, his body thrown in the lake, his great city lying in ruins.

A Supreme Case of Syncretism

When the Spaniards arrived at the great Tenochtitlan, the heart of the Aztec Empire, Emperor Montezuma II was allied with two other kingdoms, Texcoco and Tlacopan, known as the Triple Alliance. The confederation dominated the southern half of modern Mexico, from the Pacific to the Gulf shores. The progressive conquests of these territories gave Europeans access to the Pacific Ocean and, what Columbus had intended in the first place three decades before, a coveted route to the Far East. In the next century, marching from Tenochtitlan to the north, the Spanish captains would absorb more portions of the territory, as far away as California and Texas, with the unexpected "help" of the most effective biological weapon: germs.

The diseases of Europe, which were unknown in America, traveled faster than the Spanish expeditions. As the 16th century progressed, the new viceroyalty and the future Mexican Republic would be known as New Spain, a colossal territory that spread from Mexico City to

Oregon and Central America. Little has been said about the role of African slaves in the Spanish-Aztec war. As early as 1537, just fifteen years after the fall of Tenochtitlan, there were ten thousand Africans in Mexico, some of whom briefly rebelled and appointed a black king. However, his royal dream was ephemeral—after a few days of wearing his crown, he was captured and publicly executed.

The indigenous cultures did not fade away into oblivion with the Spanish occupation. One of the most characteristic symbols of Mexico, the image of the Virgin of Guadalupe, with both its indigenous and European elements, has its dark origins in the first years immediately after the fall of Tenochtitlan when there were still ruins and people who remembered the lake red with the blood of the dead. The tradition says that in 1531, the Virgin Mary appeared to a Native American named Juan Diego in the surroundings of Mexico City, on the slopes of a hill where there was previously a temple dedicated to Tonantzin, the mother of the gods. There, the Native Americans made offerings and came from faraway lands with presents. Juan Diego was a survivor of one of the most violent cultural confrontations in the history of mankind. A poem composed in those years by the survivors said, "And all this happened to us. We saw it, we observed it. With this mournful and sad fate we found ourselves in anguish. On the roads lie broken arrows, the hairs are scattered. The houses are roofless, their walls are blood-red." It was in this context of colossal loss that the image of Guadalupe emerged.

According to the legend, the Virgin told Juan Diego during her first appearance to go to Bishop Zumárraga and ask him to build a temple for her on that site. In one of the oldest chronicles written in Nahuatl, the Virgin Mary says:

I want very much that they build my sacred little house here...because I am truly your compassionate mother, yours and of all the people who live together in this land, and of all the other people of different ancestries, those who love me, those who cry to me, those who seek me, those who trust in me, because there I will listen to their weeping, their sadness, to remedy, to cleanse and nurse all their different troubles, their miseries, their suffering.

Juan Diego ignored the identity of that "beloved maiden," and he went to the bishop to tell him what he had seen on the hill. The priest did not believe him. In the third and last apparition, the image of the Virgin Mary became adhered to the *tilma* of the humble Native American as a proof for the bishop, and this same piece of cloth is still venerated today in the Basilica of Guadalupe in Mexico City, which is the most visited Catholic sanctuary in the world after the Vatican. It would not be an exaggeration to say that the image of Guadalupe—whose cult rapidly spread among Native Americans and Spaniards—was the first element of a union, which eventually transformed into a nation.

Historical fact or pious legend, most Mexicans do not take the story lightly. Until recently, a saying circulated in Mexico that said there were only two things that were untouchable: the president and the Virgin of Guadalupe. Most historians believe that the story was invented by the Franciscans. Anthropologists point out that stories do not come from nothing and that a historical core must lie behind the embellished legend. What no one questions is that the Virgin of Guadalupe has been the most important religious and political symbol in Mexico's history, a kind of unofficial flag. Its influence has extended even to the Mexican diaspora, where it is a sign of identity, pride, and struggle among undocumented immigrants in the United States. For Mexicans, it is not necessary to be religious to believe in the power of the Virgin of Guadalupe as a representative of Mexicanness and as a banner of their most important struggles, as will be seen later.

Another Colonial Jewel: Chapultepec Castle

From the colonial era comes another of Mexico City's most distinctive icons: the Castle of Chapultepec, which is, to date, the only genuine castle in the Americas, then located in the outskirts of Mexico City. In 1783, Viceroy Matías de Gálvez, who is fondly remembered for his love for the Native Americans, came up with the idea of building a new palace for the transfer of powers among viceroys. Viceroy Gálvez died suddenly without seeing his dream come true, but he had sown the idea. It would fall upon his son Bernardo to complete the castle. Bernardo Gálvez was an experienced soldier who was a key ally of the American Revolution—the city of Galveston, Texas, is named after him—and had great sympathy for the Mexican people. He was so popular among the Mexicans that the Spanish Crown distrusted him. The first stone for the castle was laid on November 23rd, 1785. It is intriguing to think that the intention behind Chapultepec could have been more than pure ostentation. It's probable that it was built exactly for the purpose that castles had been constructed in Europe: for military purposes, and in Mexico's case, in order to pave the way to independence.

Ideas of liberty were already running throughout the Americas, and Gálvez had a distinguished military career with many triumphs. People began frequently speaking about the building as a fortress, and there was a rumor that Gálvez had been thinking of declaring the independence of Mexico and installing his palace in Chapultepec, according to the traveler and geographer Alexander von Humboldt, who visited New Spain in 1804. If that was indeed the case, then the king of Spain was not so wrong to harbor suspicions and order the interruption of the castle's construction the following year. The beloved Viceroy Gálvez died in 1786, and Chapultepec was abandoned for many years. But a lot of history was going to happen on that hill in the following two centuries.

Chapter 3 – The Birth of a Nation

"All former Spanish colonies are now in insurrection. What kind of government will they establish? How much liberty can they bear without intoxication? Are their chiefs sufficiently enlightened to form a well-guarded government, and their people to watch their chiefs? Have they mind enough to place their domesticated Indians on a footing with the whites?"

—Thomas Jefferson to Alexander von Humboldt in April 1811

The colonial era under the dominion of the Spanish Empire lasted for three centuries. Between 1521, when Tenochtitlan capitulated, and 1821, when Mexico signed its act of independence, New Spain increased its power from Lake Texcoco in every geographical direction to form a colossal country of almost five million square kilometers. The Spaniards, hoping to find gold and silver, went north and south, conquering and subjugating peoples until they reached as far as Panama in the south and the center of the United States in the north. The stories about El Dorado, a city made of gold, and the Fountain of Youth, tales that were propagated by the Spaniards, encouraged more expeditions in search of mythical kingdoms. Only the unruly peninsula of Yucatan and the Mayas remained in constant insurrection for centuries, composing an impenetrable and fiercely independent zone.

The Kingdom of New Spain, part of the Habsburg Empire, came to include modern-day Mexico, the American states of California, Nevada, Colorado, Utah, New Mexico, Arizona, Texas, Oregon, Washington, Florida, and parts of Idaho, Montana, Wyoming, Kansas, Oklahoma, Alabama, Mississippi, and Louisiana. It also included the modern countries of Central America, the Philippines, Guam, and other islands. However, like everything in the American continent at the time, these borders were unstable. The Spanish conquests responded—besides the crave for gold—to France's expansionism in the east and Russia in the west, which led Spain to populate the Pacific Coast up to California with missions and towns.

During the colonial period, a very high mortality rate due to European diseases, forced labor, and war resulted in a real catastrophe for the native population. When Cortés met Montezuma, the land that would become New Spain had a population of about twenty million inhabitants; in three centuries, this figure dropped to six million. On the other hand, with the arrival of more Spaniards to America, including women, the European and the indigenous population intermarried and formed the mestizo population, which predominates to this day in Mexico, although it should be mentioned that Native Americans, such as the Maya and the northern tribes, resisted assimilation. This is the reason why Mexico still has some of its original population. In the last years of New Spain, a census ordered by Viceroy Revillagigedo revealed that there were 60 percent indigenous, 22 percent mestizos, 18 percent white, and a minimal number of African Americans. The whites—including the clergy—owned almost all property.

Although libertarian ideas were already running throughout New Spain, it was not until 1810 that a priest named Miguel Hidalgo managed to gather a crowd early in the morning of September in a small village in central Mexico. Armed with sticks, hoes, and a few rusty guns, people started a revolution that would last, with intermittence, more than a decade. His first pronouncements were against political and economic subordination. "My friends and compatriots," Hidalgo shouted, "there is no longer for us neither king nor taxes; this shameful gavel, which only suits slaves, we have endured for three centuries as a sign of tyranny and servitude; a terrible stain that we will know how to wash with our struggle. The time has come for our emancipation; the hour of our freedom has sounded; and if you know its great value, you will help me defend it from the ambitious grip of tyrants." But the first revolutionaries were not actually seeking total independence from Spain. They were rebelling against Napoleon's occupation of Spain. Or at least that was their alibi.

Before Father Hidalgo, there had been sporadic Native American rebellions, African slave riots, miners' strikes, and protests over hunger. On more than one occasion, the battle cry "Death to the bad government!" had been voiced. The column that followed Father Hidalgo, which was more similar to an angry, murderous mob than a true army, carried a banner that can be considered Mexico's first flag: a representation of the Virgin of Guadalupe, an image venerated in Mexico City shortly after the fall of Tenochtitlan, a symbol that Hidalgo knew appealed to all social classes and could attract everyone, Native Americans and whites. Hidalgo and his men captured a few minor cities. However, his ardent and apparently unstoppable rebellion was stifled by the superior Spanish forces after their first successes in central Mexico. It was too late, though, as Hidalgo's call echoed through all the land. Another priest named José María Morelos, a rude military man from the south, embraced the cause. Morelos was a brown-skinned, short, and stocky determined man, who always wore a headscarf moistened with medicinal herbs because he suffered from migraines.

The leaders of the independence movement proclaimed Morelos "Most Serene Highness"—a title that Father Hidalgo had adopted for himself— but the Morelos vehemently rejected it and preferred to be called "Servant of the Nation." This was more than politics or diplomacy. Morelos was a true revolutionary. When they showed him a draft of the constitution for the new nation, where the freedom of Mexico was stipulated but sovereignty still resided in the Spanish king, Fernando (Ferdinand) VII, Morelos raised his glass and exclaimed, "Long live Spain, but a sister Spain, not one dominating America." Morelos also got rid of the image of the Virgin as a flag for the insurgents and, for the first time, placed the image of an eagle on a cactus.

Morelos, unlike Hidalgo, was a true soldier. Upon learning of his military genius, Napoleon Bonaparte allegedly said, "Give me three Morelos and I will conquer the world." The skillful priest became the soul of the Mexican War of Independence. Among his innovations was the creation of a children's battalion that helped him in his most important battles. When under siege in Cuautla, a town in southern Mexico, the rebels fled, fearing the imminent attack. Only one boy named Narciso Mendoza stood still, facing the column charging against him. Mechanically, the twelve-year-old boy took a torch and lit up a loaded cannon with its mouth directed toward the street where the royalist column was coming. This unexpected and fearless action allowed the revolutionaries to return to their positions and restore order. Morelos assigned the boy a salary throughout the campaign.

In 1813, Morelos presented a document called *Feelings of the Nation*, a kind of proto-constitution for the new country. Morelos decreed the abolition of slavery and the elimination of the legal figure of the king of Spain; laws were also issued to eliminate poverty and limit wealth, jobs would be reserved for the Americans (this is, not for Europeans), and it decreed an end for the payment of tributes. As a form of government, unlike most of the leaders of the revolution, Morelos believed in a brand-new republic, free from its past. "It is lawful for a conquered kingdom to reconquer itself, and for an obedient kingdom it is lawful not to obey the king, when the king is oppressive in his laws."

By the middle of the 1810s, the independence revolution came to a stall. Both Hidalgo and Morelos had been arrested, tried by the Inquisition, declared heretics, excommunicated, and finally executed by the judicial authority. The new viceroy offered a pardon to the rebels, which many accepted, and by 1819, New Spain seemed to be at peace. A few minor *caudillos* (military or political leaders) barely survived in the mountains, but they continued the fight, and a few shots were heard here and there. One of those insurgents, Guadalupe Victoria, who would become the first president of Mexico, spent several years hiding in a cave. The revolution, weakened but with a spark of life, was left to Vicente Guerrero, a rebel from the south, who would become the second president of Mexico and the first African American president in the Americas. The viceroy of New Spain sent Guerrero's father to ask him, for the good of all, to surrender and accept the pardon. Guerrero received his father, listened to him, and then sent him away with a saying that people still remember: "*La Patria es primero*"— "The Motherland first." Things took a favorable turn as the new decade set in when the commander of the royalist forces of the south, Agustín de Iturbide, who was sent to crush Vicente Guerrero, instead became an ally. Together, they launched the Plan of Iguala, where they declared Mexico to be an independent, Catholic country and the home of Spaniards, Creoles (Mexican-born whites of Spanish heritage), Native Americans, blacks, and mestizos alike. With this alliance, the Spanish authorities realized that their cause was lost. Agustín de Iturbide marched into the capital on September 27th, 1821, and thus began the life of independent Mexico.

At this time, the name "Mexico" emerged to refer to the whole nation that would replace New Spain. During the colonial period, and since the times of the Spanish-Aztec war, the word Mexico appears in several documents but only in reference to Tenochtitlan and its sphere of influence. The whole territory was known as "America,"

"North America," "Mexican America" (in the first constitution), and "Anahuac" (pronounced *Anawak*), a name given by the Mexica to the world known to them. Anahuac means "the land completely surrounded by water" or, more formally, "the totality of what is between the waters." By Anahuac, they meant everything known between the Pacific and the Atlantic Oceans. The priest José María Morelos referred to the country as the Anahuac Republic. One of the most interesting references that anticipated the name that Mexico would adopt appeared in the *Texas Gazette* on May 25th, 1813, where it is called the "United States of Mexico." Finally, in 1816, the term "Mexican Republic" came up during the Mexican War of Independence to replace that of "New Spain." The flag of that republic, which did not exist yet except in the mind of the insurgents, was an eagle devouring a snake standing on a cactus in a lake. The country was embracing its indigenous past. The republic's official name became the "United Mexican States," which remains to this day. Although the whole world and its own inhabitants call it simply "Mexico," as of 2020, it is not yet the official name of the country.

Mexico declared itself independent in 1821, exactly three centuries later—minus one month—after the fall of Tenochtitlan. Spain lost all of its rights over New Spain, and Mexico began its own life as a monarchy. The annexation of the Captaincy General of Guatemala, which included all of Central America, was received gladly. The first emperor of Mexico was Agustín de Iturbide, and he was crowned on July 21st, 1822, inside the Cathedral of Mexico City in a remarkably original ceremony due to its novelty and the constitutional character of the ruler. It was an "inauguration, consecration and coronation" of a monarch, something unheard of; even more, Iturbide was also a "constitutional emperor." In the ceremony, which was meticulously prepared by the deputies in terms of symbolism and location of the attendees, Congress added several gestures to show that, contrary to Napoleon's, this would be a constitutional empire. It was Congress, not God, the pope, or a monarch, who put the crown on the emperor's head. Many saw the ceremony as a form of personal legitimation of Iturbide through the Church, but it actually was a somewhat different project, as Iturbide had not prepared the ritual. The members of Congress actually arranged the ceremony, and they were already positioning the legal body to be Iturbide's future rival.

Iturbide thus inherited a mammoth country that would have aroused the envy of Alexander the Great himself. From Panama in the south to the limits of Oregon in the north, it was almost five thousand miles from side to side, or five million square kilometers, which was greater than Alexander's empire. However, the only impressive thing about Mexico was its size: many territories were just wilderness and not much more. The task of building a country was just beginning, and for Mexico—which, since the first day, was divided into uncompromising factions—it would not be an easy task. In fact, in the following years, it would come close to disintegrating and dissolving. "I cannot imagine a worst punishment to Mexicans," said Spanish Mayor Miguel Bataller in the first years of the Mexican War of Independence, "than to let them govern themselves." The following decades apparently proved him right.

Chapter 4 – "From the Halls of Montezuma..."

"The insatiable ambition of the United States,

favored by our own weakness, caused that war."

Guillermo Prieto, 1847

Modern Mexico was born with problems. After eleven years of war, many parts of the country were in ruins; roads, buildings, and dams were destroyed, and the countryside was abandoned. The institutions had been dismantled, and two pressing problems would be the country's plague throughout the rest of the century: the bankruptcy of public finances and political divisions. The national treasury was empty, and future revenues were already committed. The empire of Agustín de Iturbide barely lasted a year before an internal rebellion deposed him. He was succeeded by Guadalupe Victoria—literally "Guadalupe Victory"—who became the first president. This was not his real name but one adopted in honor of the Virgin of Guadalupe and the victory over the Spaniards. Victoria, who had fought in the Mexican War of Independence, was succeeded by Vicente Guerrero, who was the first president of African American descent in the continent. Guerrero immediately decreed the liberation of black slaves and the permanent prohibition of slavery, which was a more symbolic gesture in central Mexico but one that would have acute repercussions in the north, where there were still slaves, specifically in Tejas (later Texas), which at that time was part of Mexico.

The government of Vicente Guerrero, the liberator of slaves, barely lasted for eight months before he was deposed by another rebellion. The third president could not achieve much either, as José María Bocanegra lasted for only one week. The next one, Anastasio Bustamante, was also deposed by a rebellion. This established a terrible precedent of what politics in Mexico would be like. Virtually all of the following presidents, until the end of the century, would be expelled by coups. That instability had immediate consequences on the territory that had once been New Spain. The first ones to say goodbye were the provinces of Central America (the modern countries of Guatemala, El Salvador, Honduras, Nicaragua, and Costa Rica). The state of Chiapas was next when it declared independence in 1823, then followed Yucatan.

The Republic of Yucatan

With Emperor Agustín de Iturbide gone, a rebel soldier named Antonio López de Santa Anna, a character who would give many headaches to Mexico in the following decades, tried to take the crown. However, instead of assuming the royal title of Antonio I as he wished, he was sent to be the governor of the farthest place in the country, Yucatan, the poorest state in the republic. It was almost equivalent to exile.

At that time, the only way to reach the peninsula, the home of the Maya and the old center of the pre-Columbian empire, was by sea. Far from Mexico City, Yucatan made a living off its commercial relations with the Caribbean—especially the vibrant city of Havana. Governor Santa Anna realized that the merchants and principal men in Yucatan felt closer to Spain than to Mexico as they even referred to Mexico as if it was another country. Yucatan's economy was supported by its trade with the Spanish colonies. The problem was that Mexico had ordered the governors to suspend trade with Spain and its colonies, including Cuba, which meant cutting off Yucatan's main source of income. The ruling class in the peninsula wanted to backpedal their independence and rejoin the Spanish Empire or, as a matter of choice, to declare itself a separate republic.

Santa Anna asked the federal government to lift the ban on trade with Cuba, but the central government frowned at the request. Santa Anna concluded—displaying his ability to think on a grand scale that he demonstrated his whole life—that the only way to help Yucatan would be to make Cuba independent and annex it to Mexico. With that purpose in mind, he would lead a liberating expedition. He assembled five thousand men and cleared the decks to leave in August 1824. According to his calculations, the inhabitants of the island would welcome him as a hero. However, Spain learned about his plans and fortified the island. Also, the government of Mexico, under diplomatic pressure from the United States and Great Britain, which did not wish to alter the balance in the Caribbean, pulled Santa Anna's ear. Without patronage or protection from anyone, what could have been an interesting chapter in Mexico's life was left aside.

Texas and the Alamo

Mexico extended for almost five million square kilometers but had only six million inhabitants, most of them crowding the south-center of the country. The nation's population density was 1.2 inhabitants per square kilometer, which was three times less than 19th-century Canada or Australia. It was practically an invitation to be invaded, and more regions began threatening to separate. The former New Spain, which had encompassed a territory superior to that of all of Western Europe, was facing the grim prospect of disintegrating. The separation of Central America had occurred without a single shot, and Yucatan was so far from everything that it was probably costlier to bring it into line than losing it.

Emperor Iturbide had been worried about distant Tejas since the beginning, as Spain had not made efforts to colonize it. Few people wanted, however, to move to Texas, although the government offered help to colonize its lands. There were good reasons for not wanting to take the family to Texas: the place was in the region of the Apaches, Comanches, Wichitas, Caddos, Tonkawas, Cherokees, and Karankawas, peoples that the Spanish had been unable to subdue. They were fierce, lionhearted warriors, stocked with horses and weapons. In 1835, the Mexican government intensified hostilities and even offered 100 pesos for each Apache scalp older than fourteen, 50 pesos for each woman's scalp, and 25 pesos per child.

In Tejas, the Mexican government donated land, granted tax exemptions, and allowed the free import of any item necessary for the colony. These were such exceptional conditions that US Secretary of State Henry Clay commented, "Little interest the Mexicans must have in keeping Texas, since they are giving it away!" In 1825, Stephen Austin arrived in the region after gaining the permission of the governor of Tejas, Antonio Martínez. Austin's first three hundred Anglo families came with their slaves. Mexico had granted them permission to enter on the condition that they swore allegiance to the country and brought no slaves, but Texas was too far away to enforce these laws. Not ten years had passed, and the Anglo-Saxon population—which consisted of well-educated, fairly well-off Protestants with an entrepreneurial, pioneering spirit—was three times larger than the Hispanics. Coexistence, unfortunately, was not amicable. Anglo-Saxon citizens (at that time, though, they were officially Mexicans) called Hispanics "greasers" because they thought their brown skin looked like dirt and because they fried their food in lard. It was also taboo for the Anglo-Saxon citizens to mix with Hispanic or mestizo families. Some began to see Mexicans as less than human and expendable, and the same went for Native Americans and blacks. Creed Taylor, a migrant who joined the Texas Revolution when he was fifteen, later recalled, "I thought I could shoot Mexicans just like Indians, or deer or turkeys, that's why I joined the war."

When Vicente Guerrero abolished slavery, the shockwaves came as an earthquake to Stephen Austin's colony, which already had eight thousand people. A quarter of them were black slaves. Being so distant, as Tejas was nine hundred miles away, there was little Mexico could do except increase its military presence and try to enforce the law. An 1830 report by an official envoy recommended the government suspend new entry permits, allow the arrival of citizens from Germany, Switzerland, and Mexico to curtail American influence, and finish the grace period without paying taxes. Austin's settlers began to conspire. In Mexico's capital, it was no longer a secret that conflict was brewing. When the Anglo-Saxons expelled the Hispanic Mexicans and declared themselves independent in 1836, Santa Anna, who first became president in 1833, left the presidential chair in a fury to go himself to crush the Texan separatists. When Santa Anna's troops arrived at El Alamo, an old fortress and mission built by the Spaniards in the 18th century, his men informed him that many Texan rebels had taken refuge there. According to some testimonies, the Mexican Army first sent a messenger with a white flag to offer the defenders an opportunity to surrender. Before the envoy could knock on the Alamo's door, William Travis, the man in charge, shot him. The act angered the Mexicans, who planted a red flag, meaning there would be no prisoners. The rebels had been declared as "pirates," and, therefore, deserved the death penalty. There were heavy casualties on both sides, who fought courageously. This dramatic clash, and the killing of prisoners in Fort Goliad, turned the Texas Revolution into a racial conflict. Santa Anna was captured days later when Sam Houston's soldiers surprised him in a poorly planned encampment, but instead of killing him, they took him to Houston, who made him a prisoner for several months.

The Texas Revolution is surrounded by folk tales and stories of heroism. One of the more colorful episodes, which does have a historical basis, although the details differ from one version to another, happened when General Santa Anna was a prisoner. One of the Texan soldiers saw him chewing a tree resin that the general was carrying among his belongings, and he asked what it was. Santa Anna replied that it was called chewing gum. The soldier, named Adams, remembered the information, and years later, he added sugar and colors and launched the multi-million dollar chewing gum industry alongside William Wrigley. Meanwhile, in Mexico, the military left Santa Anna alone as a prisoner of Houston. Eternally divided, the intrigues and betrayals in the capital resulted in Mexico losing the Provincia de Tejas, which proclaimed its independence in 1836 and became the Republic of Texas. Given that Chiapas and Yucatan eventually returned to the fold, the Lone Star State was the only one in Mexico that successfully separated through an armed revolt to become an independent country, although it did have the help of the United States.

Encouraged by Texas's example, the winds of independence once again blew in Yucatan, especially when Mexico decreed that the states would lose their sovereignty to become departments; their governors would be appointed in the capital and would lose their state militias. Yucatan took this occasion to separate for a second time. In retaliation, in 1841, the Mexican government blocked the ports of the peninsula. The governor of Yucatan symbolically ordered the removal of all the flags of Mexico and to raise the banner of the new republic. Yucatan's flag was vaguely reminiscent of the flag of the United States: a green field to symbolize independence, with red and white stripes, plus five stars representing the five divisions of the peninsula: Mérida, Izamal, Valladolid, Tekax, and Campeche.

Like Texas, Yucatan had an extensive coast in the Gulf of Mexico and thus had a direct connection with Texas by the sea without having to go inland. Therefore, both republics established relations and signed treaties of friendship and commerce. There was a diplomatic representation of Texas in Mérida and one of Yucatan in Austin. The president of Texas, Mirabeau B. Lamar, secretly negotiated an alliance against Mexico with Yucatan. For the Lone Star Republic, this was not just an altruistic move toward Yucatan: its own independent life was still fragile. While Mexico remained busy trying to suffocate the separatist attempts in the peninsula, it would leave Texas alone. Yucatan agreed to pay eight thousand dollars a month to Texas to defend the Yucatec coast from Mexican attacks, and both republics agreed that if there were any loot from the ships they captured, they would divide the spoils equally. Although Texan ships briefly patrolled the Yucatec coast, they never faced Mexico. However, isolated and endangered in the face of international and internal conflicts, a few years later, Yucatan recognized the need to rejoin Mexico and went back with its tail tucked between its metaphorical legs.

More urgent problems were brewing in the north. When the United States recognized Texas's independence, and a few years later even approved the annexation of the young republic, thus becoming the 28th state of the American Union, Mexico considered it a provocation. Despite the vehement recommendations of the British government, Mexican generals began to demand some kind of punishment. The words of the English proved to be prophetic. When Texas declared that the Rio Grande would be its new border, some 200 kilometers (a little over 124 miles) farther south than originally agreed, tensions broke out. The United States had previously offered to buy Texas and California from Mexico, but the latter had always refused. US President James K. Polk, an expansionist who had almost gone to war against Britain over Oregon, offered between twenty and forty million dollars for California and New Mexico. At the same time, Polk sent armed forces to the border, hoping to make a point, as well as hoping that Mexico would yield in the face of intimidation. In March of 1846, American troops crossed the international border, which was marked by the Nueces River, and continued on until they reached the Rio Grande. This was a clear provocation since it was a region inhabited by Mexican families. When Mexico demanded them to withdraw, the first incident exploded. In Washington, DC, President Polk shouted from the rooftops that Mexico had shed American blood on American soil, which was false. With his goal accomplished, the US government quickly declared war against its weak southern neighbor.

The result of the Mexican-American War was predictable. At the beginning of the conflict, the United States had 22 million inhabitants, Mexico less than 7 million. The former had a buoyant economy and a powerful industrial base, while Mexico was bankrupt and, even in the midst of war, brimming with divisions. Instead of uniting against a common enemy, Mexicans continued with their eternal divisions and even planned more revolutions. Many state governors, mixing their priorities, refused to send troops to help with the war effort. Yucatan declared itself neutral, and others promoted rebellions against the presidents—incredibly, Mexico had seven presidents between 1846 and 1848, the years of war against the United States. The local chiefs left the federal government by itself, with obsolete weapons and improvised generals, to defend a huge semi-uninhabited territory against an industrial giant. The Mexican soldiers were mostly peasants recruited against their will, and they were poorly fed and demoralized to see how the wounded were abandoned on the battlefield. By January 1847, the United States had already annexed the Mexican provinces of New Mexico and California, as well as other parts of the country. The Texas Rangers, at this point in history famous for their indiscipline, and still seeking vengeance for the Alamo, massacred countless civilians in Monterrey.

This does not mean that Mexico did not fight to almost heroic levels with what little it had. In the middle of the war, the charismatic General Santa Anna returned. Exiled in Cuba, the former president learned about the military and political disaster in his country. Surprisingly, it was the Americans who went to ask for his help. Santa Anna received President Polk's envoy, a colonel named Alexander Atocha, who offered to ship him to Mexico with the promise that the United States would support him to be, once again, Mexico's president as long as he agreed to sell the desired territories to the US. Santa Anna gave the go-ahead. Believing that he had just created a traitor to his country and won an ally for the US, Polk sent a confidential letter to the commander of the US Gulf Squad, telling him to let Santa Anna pass unmolested if he tried to enter Mexico.

However, as soon as he set foot in Veracruz on September 12th, 1846, the US realized that Santa Anna had tricked them. A small crowd gathered to receive him as a hero as soon as they heard he was back. "Mexicans! There was a day when you greeted me with the title of Soldier of the People," Santa Anna addressed the group. "Let me take it again and devote myself even to the death in defense of the freedom and independence of the republic!" He quickly assembled an army from nowhere in San Luis Potosí and marched north to hold back General Zachary Taylor's unstoppable advance. On the outskirts of the city of Saltillo, the armies met. Santa Anna gave Taylor the chance to surrender. "Illustrious Sir," he wrote, "you are surrounded by 20,000 men and cannot in any human probability avoid suffering a rout, and being cut to pieces with your troops, but as you deserve consideration and particular esteem, I wish to save you from a catastrophe." When Taylor read the letter, he shouted, "Tell Santa Anna to go to hell! Put that in Spanish and send it to him!"

It was then that one of the fiercest battles of the Mexican-American War took place. Santa Anna, the one-legged soldier, emboldened his soldiers and rode like lightning among his troops. A testimony of the time pictured him this way:

He gallops from one position to another, despite the pain he suffers in his incomplete leg, indifferent to the grenades exploding around him. A horse falls dead and he falls to the ground, he stands up, takes another horse and continues running through the field with his sword drawn and waving only a small whip. Behind him, an aide-de-camp gallops to convey his orders. Soldiers are inspired by his example of courage, and during these hours of emotion, he reached perhaps the most honorable point of his career.

Incredibly, Santa Anna got a victory, but even more disconcerting to historians is the fact that after the heroic win, he withdrew from the battlefield, apparently because his troops could no longer go on. But the blunder was too much for the United States, which decided to open a second front in the Gulf of Mexico, where General Winfield Scott followed the route that three centuries earlier Cortés had taken toward the great Tenochtitlan. Scott began the attack on the capital in September 1847, which was the last line of resistance. At the gates of Mexico City, the church bells, which had been silent for days, rang like a siren. A dramatic and fierce battle ensued. Even the civilian population, who had been terrified as they hid in their houses, went outside or climbed to the rooftops to attack the invaders, including women and children. Mexico's government, which was now on the run, opened up the jails and released all the prisoners to join the battle.

On September 16th, on the anniversary of Mexican independence, the Stars and Stripes waved over the National Palace of Mexico City. Meanwhile, in the United States, many in Washington asked for the complete annexation of Mexico. The White House recalled Nicholas Trist, President Polk's envoy to negotiate peace, to receive new instructions and ask for more land, including the Lower California Peninsula, the Yucatan Peninsula, and the Isthmus of Tehuantepec, the thin strip of land where the Pacific and the Gulf of Mexico are closest. Trist was in a dilemma because he had already made progress in his negotiations and refused to return to Washington. Years later, Trist would confess to his family the shame that had overwhelmed him "during all the conferences, in the face of the unjust war." With the signing of the Treaty of Guadalupe-Hidalgo in February 1848, the territory of Mexico was reduced by half. After the partition, many Mexicans were left behind in the former provinces of what would become California, New Mexico, and Texas. Despite suffering abuse for many years, they managed to survive with their culture and traditions in a hostile environment. Their descendants were called "Chicanos"—a derivation of the Nahuatl word "Meshico"—and they still live in the southern United States, where they have become an increasingly relevant cultural, political, and economic presence.

Chapter 5 – The Big Division

Before losing half of its territory, Mexicans did not have much of a common identity. If the trauma of war and mutilation had any positive consequences, it was that people from different regions, from Baja California to Yucatan, began to realize that they shared a common history and destiny. Santa Anna, to whom practically the first period of independent Mexico belonged—to such an extent that those decades are known as "Santa Anna's Mexico"—became president once again in 1853, twenty years after his first inauguration. "Everything expects a remedy from General Santa Anna. Come then, as it has been announced, to your mission of saving Mexico from its ruins," published a newspaper of the time.

Despite suffering from territorial indigestion that would eventually lead to its own civil war, the United States continued to press Mexico for more land. Many voices in the north called for a complete annexation. In the next decade, the United States opened new claims on the border, given that its planned transcontinental train to the Pacific had to pass necessarily through Mexican soil since the American side was very mountainous. James Gadsden, the ambassador to Mexico, met with Santa Anna and showed him a map with the border that his country desired; it included not only the relatively small portion of land where the train should pass, but it also had an international line that was much farther south. In view of the occasion, Gadsden had fixed the line so that the peninsula of Baja California and the Mexican states of Sonora, Sinaloa, Durango, and Chihuahua would pass into the domain of the United States. If Mexico were to agree to this demand, its territory would once again be cut in half. A band of adventurers had just failed in their attempt to annex Baja California and Sonora to the United States, and it was as if the Texas situation was happening all over again. Santa Anna realized that the US was willing to go to a new war and would gladly seize another half from his country if he did not resolve the Mesilla issue soon. That was the name of the territory that the projected train would cut through, located in the modern states of Arizona and New Mexico.

The operation known as the "Gadsden Purchase" was signed in 1853; the Mexican government got 15 million dollars for 76,000 square kilometers. Thus, General Santa Anna acted with a practical sense and avoided war, but the people did not forgive him. Santa Anna, who was formerly a Liberal, became a kind of frivolous king who called himself "His Most Serene Highness"—just like Father Hidalgo in the Mexican War of Independence—and, to sustain the excesses of his extravagant court, he invented absurd taxes for the population, such as taxes on the number of windows in a house and taxes per pet, among others.

His last stay in the National Palace, however, left behind one of Mexico's distinctive marks. In 1853, Santa Anna organized a contest to choose a national anthem that would unite the Mexicans scattered across the north, south, and east. First, a contest was opened to choose the lyrics. There was a young and talented poet named Francisco González Bocanegra who did not dare to compete because he mostly wrote love poems. Bocanegra considered that a patriotic hymn was beyond his lyrical reach. As he resisted to enter the competition, despite his friends encouraging him to write, his girlfriend, disgusted, set him a small trap. With tricks, she walked him to an out-of-the-way room in her parents' house, pushed him inside, and immediately threw a padlock on the door, warning him that she wouldn't let him out until he wrote something. Four hours later, Francisco slipped under the door what would be the Mexican National Anthem. He won the contest by a unanimous vote.

Then the prize for the music was opened, which was appropriately won by a Spanish composer named Jaime Nunó, a director of several military bands. In this way, the two nations that had given birth to modern Mexico were founded in an anthem.

The verses of the hymn reflect the history and character of the country. With an almost apocalyptic tone, the poem is full of tragedy, rumors of war, waves of blood, strange enemies desecrating the homeland, towers and palaces crumbling down with horrid rumble, a mention of a grave, and God's implacable finger. The room in which Bocanegra was locked up held several scenes of the history of Mexico decorated on the walls, which inspired the poet to write the stanzas. The paintings must have been terrible. "O, Fatherland, ere your children, defenseless, bend their neck beneath the yoke, may your fields be watered with blood, may their foot be printed in blood. And may your temples, palaces and towers collapse with horrid clamor, and may their ruins continue on, saying: Of one thousand heroes, here the Fatherland once was."

The hymn was first performed officially on September 16th, 1854, Independence Day. The orchestra was conducted by director Jaime Nunó himself in the presence of an aged Santa Anna.

The Reform War

When a new uprising in the south overthrew Santa Anna, the eternal division between Liberals and Conservatives opened again, this time with more brutality. Liberals wanted a republic in the American style, one that was representative, federal, and popular, with separation between church and state. Above all, they wanted to expropriate the Catholic Church's property, which had great resources ever since the time of New Spain. The Church sometimes lent money to the government, and it possessed extensive assets, which, in many cases, were unproductive. The Conservatives, seeing the chaos in which the country had been in for several years, with its rebellious states and an inept and obstructive Congress that never accomplished anything, sought a strong, centralist state that was supported in the Church and the army.

The division had deep historical roots. The military disaster that ended in a defeat inflicted by the Americans sank the country in a period of dejection that permeated all aspects of social life. This situation gave rise to a self-critical examination of the national predicament and led to a renewed search for viable solutions to the problems that afflicted the country. The most eminent Conservatives proposed a change in the directions of politics, postulating the return to the old ways, and the preservation of institutions and modes of coexistence inherited from their Spanish past. Around these ideas, a conservative, oppositional, and militant party emerged with overwhelming force. The Conservatives aimed their ideological attacks to refute the Liberal doctrine, arguing that they wanted to save the country from the anarchy and ruin that, in their view, was imminent. They attributed this situation to the fact that independent Mexico had broken with its historical past to adopt government systems based on principles and institutions copied from foreign models; they postulated that Mexicans should strive to direct their efforts toward the country's reconstruction and that they should be inspired by feelings of respect for authority, religion, and property. Ultimately, after seeing uprising after uprising, as well as the gradual loss of territory, they came to propose a monarchy as the only way of salvation.

After Santa Anna's final fall, the so-called War of Reform erupted with unusual force. The country was divided between those who supported the new constitution of 1857, which decreed the freedom of religion, freedom of the press, and equality before the law, among other things, and those who opposed it. The situation was much more than political. The moment divided even families, where respect for the ecclesiastical authorities weighed against those who, like many sincere believers, considered that the Church should submit to political authority. The Reform War was not just another uprising of a rebel general to put one president in place of another. It was a revolution to define the country's direction. In the war, which was not regional but national, both sides committed unjust acts against the Church and civilians, demanding forced loans that would never be paid. Although they were defeated at the beginning, the Liberals managed to change the course of the war at the Battle of Silao in 1860. Conservatives dispersed into guerrilla factions as they continued to study how to secure the intervention of a European power.

In 1859, the Liberal president Benito Juárez had decreed the nationalization of clergy assets to pay debts to anxious foreign lenders and strengthen his government, which further aggravated the division. During the Reform War, there were two presidents, one in Veracruz and one in Mexico City, and both sides sought foreign help. Juárez offered more territory to the United States, but luckily for Mexico, the offer was rejected by the US Congress. In early 1861, Benito Juárez, who represented the new direction of the country, made his entrance into Mexico City and expelled members of the clergy, including bishops and ambassadors from countries that had not supported him. But the hostilities were far from over. From the outset, the government was still bankrupt. The value of the Church's properties had been overestimated, many assets had been wasted, and the ministers were not able to organize public finances. Much to his dismay, Juárez, with progressive ideas but an empty national treasury, was forced to suspend the payment of the external debt. The dice were cast, and Mexico's next chapter is one of the most dramatic and studied moments of its existence, despite having been brief: a monarchy. And it was just not any monarchy—it was an empire.

Chapter 6 – "The Most Beautiful Empire in the World"

"Our enemies may be the best soldiers in the world,

but you are the best children of Mexico."

Ignacio Zaragoza to his men, Battle of Puebla, Cinco de Mayo

In those days, declaring a suspension of external debt payments was no small feat, especially when the debtors were Britain, France, and Spain. France was under Napoleon III, who had promised to extend his dominion overseas, and Spain, although it had diplomatic relations with Mexico, was still distrustful toward its former colony, and it had even contemplated reconquest. As soon as President Juárez announced that he could not pay, the three nations sent their war fleets to Mexico to collectively demand, at gunpoint, the interest payments. When they arrived in Veracruz, where Hernán Cortés and Winfield Scott had landed on their way to the capital, the tripartite alliance seized the customs of the most important ports in the Gulf. The representative of Mexico met with the commission and guaranteed the Europeans that the country could and would pay.

However, one of the three countries had further intentions besides the purely financial. Napoleon III had bought into the idea that he

---

could establish a monarchy in Mexico and have an ally that would help him curb the expansion of the United States and protect the culture of Latin America—a term coined by him—from the Anglo-Saxon Protestant advance. Napoleon also had hopes on a projected canal in Nicaragua or one crossing the Isthmus of Tehuantepec. When Spain and Britain realized that the troops of Napoleon III did not plan to retire but instead march to Mexico City and take the country, they washed their hands and sailed back to Europe. An alarmed Juárez saw how a new formidable threat loomed over Mexico, while the French minister Dubois de Saligny published a manifesto to the Mexicans, where he reiterated that France harbored no bad intentions.

Mexicans, we did not come to take sides in your divisions. We have come to put an end to them. What we want is to invite all men of good will to join the consolidation of order, the regeneration of this great country. And to give proof of our sincere desire for conciliation...we have asked you to accept our help to establish a state of affairs in Mexico that prevents us from having to organize these expensive expeditions again.

When the army of the *Pantalons Rouge,* under the command of Charles de Lorencez, saw the city of Puebla in the distance, they were practically at the gates of the capital. General Lorencez wrote to Napoleon III that he had such military and human superiority over the Mexicans that he could already be considered Mexico's master. French minister Saligny assured Lorencez that the Mexicans would greet him with a shower of flowers in Puebla.

The Battle of Cinco de Mayo

Juárez was ready for the possibility of a government in exile, but first, he sent his best general to try to stop the French. Ignacio Zaragoza was born in Texas when it was still a Mexican province, and he looked more like a seminary student than a soldier. At the gates of Puebla, some recommended Lorencez to pass by and go directly to Mexico City, but there was still the Guadalupe fort on a hill to deal with, as Zaragoza's forces were waiting there, many of them peasants with moth-eaten weapons. Lorencez decided to take the city, certain that any resistance would crumble in half an hour. In the war against the United States fifteen years earlier, the Mexican Army used to withdraw amid chaos, running in panic and looting everything in its pass after a collapse. Zaragoza was careful to impose order and discipline. Many civilian volunteers showed up in the Mexican countryside to help dig trenches and lift barriers. Some asked to join the defense army, but they had to be taught how to even load a rifle.

Lorencez's plan was simple: pulverize the fortification with cannon blasts and then liquidate the survivors with the cavalry. The bell of Puebla's cathedral rang at ten o'clock in the morning when the French moved in, and the terrified citizens locked themselves in their houses. The streets became deserted. When Lorencez thought that he had broken the defense line, he charged with a column that met a shower of gunshots from the Mexicans, who not only stood firm but also threw themselves against the French. At the top of Guadalupe Hill, there ensued bloody hand-to-hand combat between Mexicans and the fierce Zouaves, a French light infantry regiment fresh from the Foreign Legion. At four o'clock in the afternoon, the French, baffled, were in retreat, and Zaragoza's cavalry went after them. When the world's most powerful army was defeated, the Mexican general telegraphed the president, "The national arms have been covered with glory." It read like something out of the national anthem. The date was May 5th, 1862.

The news was received in France with stupor. Although Napoleon would return almost a year later with a force five times greater—25,000 elite soldiers—the delay of one year in Napoleon's plans proved critical for the eventual collapse of the Mexican monarchy. Almost oblivious to this drama, at Miramar Castle in Italy, Austrian Archduke

Maximilian of Habsburg was receiving a Mexican commission that offered him the crown of Mexico. "We are lost if Europe does not come to our aid," wrote one of the most intelligent Conservatives, Lucas Alamán, and the Mexicans who went to Maximilian and his wife, Princess Charlotte of Belgium, were doing just that. They asked the couple to be the monarchs of the old Montezuma empire. They were not traitors, as later history would portray them. They actually had the sincere conviction that only a strong monarchy sponsored by a world power could save Mexico from disintegration.

The Crown of Mexico

Maximilian of Habsburg, the brother of Emperor Franz Joseph I of the Austro-Hungarian Empire, was a man of liberal ideas. He was polite, idealistic, and skeptical that Mexicans really wanted him in the country. He first demanded evidence that he would not be an imposition, and when he was presented with an alleged plebiscite with the signatures of 75 percent of Mexicans, he accepted the throne and promised that "he would establish *liberal* wise institutions and order." The Mexican commission, which was made of Conservatives, winced at those words, but it was too late to turn back. Maximilian was never completely convinced of the adventure, as it was full of risks and far from his beloved Castle of Miramar, where he liked to take care of his botanical garden, sail, and make exploratory trips around the world, but his wife Charlotte, one of the most beautiful and educated princesses in Europe, talked him into it. The most they had achieved so far was the viceroyalty of the tiny territory of Lombardy-Venice. Mexico, by comparison, was three times more extensive than the powerful Austro-Hungarian Empire of Maximilian's brother, Franz Joseph.

Charlotte, barely 23 years old, had been educated to be the head of state. She spoke French, German, Flemish, and English, and she knew about diplomacy, international politics, and even military science. What she most feared at the time, as she wrote in 1866, was to stay "to contemplate a rock until the age of sixty," referring to the cliff where the couple's castle was built. In April 1864, Maximiliano and Carlota, their adopted names for Spanish-speaking Mexico, boarded the ship to America. They stopped in Rome to receive the blessing of Pope Pius IX, heard mass in the Vatican, and then entered the Atlantic. Less than a month later, from the deck of the *Novara*, they saw the Pico de Orizaba, the highest mountain in Mexico, visible from 200 kilometers (a little over 124 miles) away. When Maximiliano touched the port of Veracruz at nine in the morning, he read a proclamation before the people who were there to welcome him. "Mexicans, you have desired me." He descended the steps and stepped on Mexican soil. It was, however, in Orizaba, 130 kilometers (almost 81 miles) inland where they were given their first formal reception and experienced real contact, which bordered on adoration, from the people. Before entering the city, the Native Americans approached the cortege, disengaged the mules from the carriage, and stood in front of it to pull it themselves along the main avenue. Maximilian flushed with embarrassment. He vehemently refused to let the Native Americans transport him as if they were beasts of burden, but they insisted so much, and the newcomers were so determined to not allow such treatment, that they had to descend and walk to Orizaba, with its streets replete with flower arcs.

Halfway to the capital, the couple made another stop in Puebla, the site of the famous battle of Cinco de Mayo, where the reception was warm. Many Mexicans, despite everything, were willing to grant them the benefit of the doubt. They had some hope that perhaps that well-intentioned rulers could stop the constant revolutions, forced recruitment, and disintegration of territory. Above all, they wanted someone to help the forgotten ones, those who had been watching all their lives as one general after another fought for the presidency: the Native Americans, the original owners of the land, who were still the majority of the country's population.

Many people in Puebla welcomed them from the balconies. Several men on horseback, along with their children, escorted them downtown. The bells rang, and the couple received a new shot of confidence. While they were in the city, Carlota (Charlotte) turned 24, and the people greeted her, but after seeing the unfortunate state of hospitals, orphanages, and schools, she corroborated what she had suspected since her arrival: that the country was destroyed after six decades of civil war. Stunned by the social disparity, Princess Carlota wrote that Mexico presented unforgivable contrasts. "If a country was ever miraculously saved from a state from which it could not emerge, I am sure it will be now." The reception in Mexico was even more enthusiastic. The historic center of Mexico City was crowded with the parade of the *Pantalons Rouge*, Napoleon's soldiers, while the new monarchs passed under flower arcs. Juárez and his government had gone into exile.

The couple was crowned in the cathedral of Mexico City on April 10th, 1864. They stayed the night in the National Palace, but the building was in a deplorable state. The first night, Maximilian had to sleep on a pool table because there were bed bugs. Soon, they found the place they were looking for. About eight kilometers (almost five miles) from the city was Chapultepec Castle, which had been built by Bernardo Gálvez on a rocky hill, although during the time of Maximilian, it was in ruins. Maximiliano, a natural optimist, set out to adapt it for his court. In a short amount of time, the old refurbished castle became the seat of the imperial government.

A Liberal Empire

In spite of many acts that the Liberals mockingly called ridiculous excesses of Maximiliano and Carlota—such as having a whole ceremony for their court and their lavish receptions at Chapultepec Castle—the monarchs were not despots nor did they lack sensitivity toward the population. Their first act was to receive a delegation of Native Americans who brought complaints about their ancestral lands. The monarchs went even further and tried to establish politics that nobody had ever dreamed of in Mexico: abolition of work for minors, freedom of worship, freedom of the press, limited workdays with two days off, the prohibition of corporal punishment, freedom to choose where to work, the obligation of employers to pay in cash (an absolute novelty), compulsory and free school for all children, the attraction of foreign scientists and technicians, the establishment of a drainage system in the cities, the planting of trees and the obligation of citizens to care for them, land property rights for peasants, freedom from peonage, and improvement of hospitals, nursing homes, and charitable houses. These measures sought to establish the basis for a liberal but human economic system, a kind of proto-social democracy.

Much less known were their plans, which were never openly expressed, to recover Central America and the Caribbean or to at least extend Mexico's sphere of influence to the south and east, establishing Yucatan as the gravitation center from which Mexico would become a continental power. But things were not going to work out for them. For a while, the empire achieved sufficient stability to be recognized by European nations, but in 1866, things started to change.

The Conservatives that had brought Maximilian were disappointed with him, as he was even more progressive than the hated Juárez. The Church and the Vatican withdrew their support because the emperor did not reverse the reform laws or restore the Church its property. And the Liberals, who supported Juárez in exile, called Maximiliano and Carlota tyrants. No one was happy with the young rulers. Even more decisive was the entry of the United States to the stage. The US had never approved European interference in the continent. Presidents Abraham Lincoln and Juárez had supported each other, and the Americans considered it inadmissible to have a monarchy sponsored by France on the other side of the Rio Grande. The US Civil War had prevented the country from intervening in Mexico and helping the Liberals. In 1866, though, things were different. Finally, Napoleon III became so overwhelmed with problems back in Paris, with the emergence of Otto von Bismarck's unified Germany, and Napoleon complained that his best generals were in Mexico. When Napoleon III announced that he was going to withdraw his troops in

America, Maximilian understood that the days of his empire were numbered.

In 1866, President Andrew Johnson helped supply Juárez and his followers with weapons and American combatants eager to do something after the end of the Civil War. Juárez's men with their foreign reinforcements and began to move south, reconquering territories, while France withdrew from Mexico. Napoleon III did not want to risk going to war with the United States. At the end of June 1866, he announced the gradual removal of his troops and advised Maximilian to abdicate. Maximilian considered the possibility of going back to Austria, but Princess Charlotte was stubbornly opposed. Desperate, seeing how they were losing more and more territory, she offered to go to Europe herself to appeal before Napoleon.

The Liberals heard of Carlota's departure to Europe, and they took it as a sign that the empire was crumbling and gained momentum. When Mexico City was being surrounded, Maximiliano's advisors urged him to leave the capital and gather his forces in Querétaro, a city that had been fortified years before by French General François Bazaine. After more than two months of hunger, siege, and gunfire, the besieged were eating horse and mule meat. Maximilian's men melted the church bells, the pipes, and all the pieces of metal they found to make ammunition. The last French soldiers left the country, and the emperor was left with a few faithful men of his Austrian guard and the remnants of the Conservative army, which was led by Miguel Miramón and Tomás Mejía. In the end, one of Maximiliano's men decided to hand over the city and let the enemy in. The emperor was arrested. After a trial, which was lost beforehand, he was sentenced to be shot on Cerro de las Campanas, located on the outskirts of the city of Querétaro.

Juárez was back in power. Although several international personalities—among them the writer Victor Hugo of *Les Misérables* fame— pleaded for Maximillian's life, Maximillian was still taken to Cerro de las Campanas on June 19th, 1867. When the emperor saw the hill, he exclaimed, "That's where I planned to unfurl the victory flag, and that's where I'm going to die. Life is a comedy!" He shook hands with each one of the soldiers who were going to shoot him. Some grieving, he comforted them by telling them that they were soldiers and should do their duty. He also handed each one a gold coin and asked them not to shoot his face so that his mother could recognize him. "I will die for a just cause" were his last words. "I forgive everyone and I also beg everyone to forgive me. May my blood seal the misfortunes of this country. Long live Mexico. *Viva Mexico!*" A few seconds later, the Austrian archduke, who had so desired for Mexico to prosper, lay dead.

And Carlota? The empress had arrived in Paris to an aging Napoleon III, begging him not to withdraw his support for Mexico. Then she went to the Vatican to kneel before the pope, trying to fix things with the Church. But at the see of San Pedro, the princess lost the battle. Her mind collapsed. Charlotte began to speak in all the languages she knew, intermingled, trembling violently, saying that Napoleon had sent assassins to kill her. Unable to hold back the tears, she begged a stunned Pope Pius IX to protect her. She immediately wrote her last letter to Maximilian, sure she had been poisoned and was going to die. But the princess did not die. Seeing that she had gone mad, her family locked her up in a castle in Belgium, where she lived for sixty more years in the darkness of insanity. In Mexico, she is still remembered with a ditty from that time: "Goodbye, Mama Carlota, goodbye, my tender love."

Chapter 7 – In the Times of Don Porfirio

"There was a Strong Man of the Americas. A dazzling future was prophesied, a golden era had arrived already, and the stock phrase was that Mexico had abandoned her turbulent, unproductive past and begun to take her rightful place among the sisterhood of nations."

—Anita Brenner

A triumphant Benito Juárez entered Mexico City on July 21ˢᵗ, 1867, accompanied by his most prominent general, Porfirio Díaz, who had recovered the capital a month earlier. This period is known as the restoration of the republic. It was the definitive triumph of the Liberals, and Juárez became the greatest hero of the republic in textbooks. Mexico City's international airport, a large city in the north of the country, and countless schools and avenues today bear his name. But in the last years of his life, when he was almost in his seventies, he clung to the presidency and provoked new uprisings in different parts of the country. Since the fall of the empire, the presidents had moved to Chapultepec Castle. Juárez considered it an excessive luxury and established his home in modest rooms in the National Palace. It was there that he died of heart disease. In his last hours, they spilled boiling water on his infarcted chest to revive him, to no avail.

The restoration of the republic did not change the country's maladies, as it suffered one uprising after another. Tired of this situation, the young general Porfirio Díaz rebelled under the Plan of Tuxtepec, which was "a revolution to end all revolutions." Díaz had been famous since the Battle of Puebla on May 5th, 1862, where he had shown fearless and heroic behavior. Under his Plan of Tuxtepec, Díaz defeated the government forces, appointed an interim president, and a year later, in 1877, he became president through a legal election, which was helped by his belief in no more reelections. Ironies of life, he would become the longest-standing president in Mexico's history: he was reelected several times for a total of 33 years, effectively governing Mexico from the 19th to the early 20th century.

Porfirio Díaz Mori, who took a poor country into his hands and delivered a more advanced nation, is a controversial character. On the one hand, he achieved what the country had longed for so long and since its birth had been unable to achieve: political stability. In the first half-century of independent Mexico, only one president had completed his term peacefully. One of them, Santa Anna, had been president eleven times, at his own whim. Two presidents lasted two months in office, others lasted less than a week, and one of them only a day. Díaz stayed at the National Palace for 33 years thanks to a hard-handed policy, the rapid elimination of his opponents, and muzzling the press. Díaz achieved the long-awaited integration of the country, which was a formerly disjointed group of isolated regions. When Porfirio Díaz came to power, there was only one railroad from Veracruz to Mexico (the Cortés route), 640 kilometers (almost 398 miles) long. Transport and commerce to the rest of the country were carried on the backs of mules. At the end of this period, almost 20,000 kilometers (a little over 12,425 miles) of railroad tracks zigzagged throughout the republic. The population increased thanks to the end of the wars and advances in public health, and it passed from nine to fifteen million, the largest population since the end of the Spanish-Aztec war. With the new infrastructure in place, people of central Mexico began to migrate and populate other areas, especially the northern states.

In its first industrial revolution, foreign investments flowed to the mining industry, railroads, ports, and lucrative crops such as coffee. Díaz and his ministers were sagacious enough to clean up the country's foreign relations and ride the so-called first great wave of globalization, which occurred in the last quarter of the 19th century. For the first time in its history, Mexico became an exporting nation. No foreign power threatened the country during the Díaz dictatorship. On the contrary, Mexico established optimum commercial and diplomatic relations with the United States, Britain, Spain, and even France, whose armies Díaz had fought in Puebla on May 5th all those years ago. Porfirio Díaz was the first to meet with a president of the United States, William Taft, in El Paso-Ciudad Juárez. "You are, to my knowledge," said the old general to his neighbor, "the first US premier to visit this land."

It was an era of reconstruction, pacification, and unification but also of repression. Díaz's first objective was to pacify the country, and to achieve this, he did not hesitate to eliminate, exile, and bribe the military and many intellectuals. He also made changes in Congress to eliminate the opposition. He reconciled with the Catholic Church and the old Conservatives to keep the peace. A very weakened Church received a vital push with Díaz, who allowed it to own property again. The clergy opened up charitable congregations and confessional schools, while Díaz attended the coronation of the Virgin of Guadalupe in 1892. Through all of this, without having to abrogate Juárez's laws, the president had the clergy on his side. Consequently, the Church stopped supporting, as it had done in the past, rebellions that were launched for the alleged defense of religion. With the Porfirian peace, the arts flourished with important people such as the poets Amado Nervo and Manuel Gutiérrez Nájera, the artists José

Guadalupe Posada and Saturnino Herrán, the composer Juventino Rosas, and the novelist Ignacio Manuel Altamirano. Díaz seemed to have achieved what his predecessors had missed: a healthy balance between the Conservatives and the Liberals.

But not everything was rosy. Notwithstanding all the new infrastructure, most of the railroads, ports, mines, and haciendas were controlled by foreign investors who had gotten very generous concessions. The United States, in particular, seemed to be taking over Mexico with abusive conditions. There was no need to swallow more territory with this new form of conquest. Díaz himself acknowledged the situation when he uttered a famous remark that Mexicans still repeat: "Poor Mexico! So far from God and so close to the United States." Agriculture flourished but only in export crops whose demand was increasing in the international markets, such as coffee, rubber, and henequen. Instead, the production of goods for the common people, which included corn, beans, wheat, and chili, decreased, and families began to starve. Inequality and the concentration of wealth increased. Large coffee, henequen, and rubber corporations absorbed communal lands and created a new caste of eternally indebted peasants.

One of the least remembered aspects of the Porfiriato, the name given to Porfirio Díaz's dictatorship, was the fierce repression of indigenous peoples, especially the Yaqui in Sonora and the Maya in Yucatan. It was around this time that a rebellion broke out in the Yucatan Peninsula, one different from all the previous indigenous wars. The life of the Mayas had not improved since the time of the Spanish conquest; indeed, it had only worsened.

The Caste War

The Mayas in Yucatan were a fiercely independent people that the Spanish had never been able to control. Since the colonial era, they had resisted white authority in many ways. In the second half of the 19th century, their situation was unbearable. The capitalist production of henequen, also known as sisal, on large haciendas only aggravated their situation. Henequen was a lucrative agave crop whose fibers were used to make ropes for boats, fabric, sacks, and other items that had a robust demand. American journalist John Kenneth Turner visited the haciendas in Yucatan at the time of Díaz and was horrified by what he saw. According to Turner, slavery persisted in Yucatan, if not officially called that in practice. "I didn't see worse punishments than beatings [on the Mayas] in Yucatan," he wrote. "Women are required to kneel to be beaten, as sometimes are men of great weight. Men and women are beaten in the fields as well as at the morning roll call. Each foreman, or capata, carries a heavy cane with which he punches and prods and whacks the slaves at will. I do not remember visiting a single field in which I did not see some of this punching and prodding and whacking going on."

The Mayas could not take it anymore and began the Caste War in 1847. It started out in a village near Mérida, where several Mayas, who were provided with food and weapons, gathered at the house of a leader named Jacinto Pat. The plan was to slaughter all the whites, proclaim the independence of the Maya, and crown a man called Cecilio Chi as their king. The authorities discovered the conspiracy, and after arresting and executing the rebels, they burned the town of Tepich, without letting women, the elderly, and children leave. The next day, Chi's men killed all the whites and mestizos, leaving only a few women behind in order to rape them, more out of hate than pleasure.

The Caste War became a war of mutual extermination, where the Mayas effectively sought to nullify the Spanish conquest, expel all the whites, and proclaim themselves autonomous and sovereign under their old laws and customs. What began as a local phenomenon became a racial war that spread throughout the Yucatan Peninsula and lasted more than half a century. When the rebels took a town or village, they slaughtered the population, and it was common for them to kill men with machetes, even when they had guns at hand. In retaliation, Mayan homes were burned by the government forces.

The white Yucatec, once again, went to the United States to seek help and protection, which they were not obtaining from Mexico. One of the principal men in Mérida, Justo Sierra O'Reilly, met with President James K. Polk in Washington, DC, and urged him to send help since the Mayas were in a war of extermination against the white population and very close to accomplishing it. The whites and mestizos in Yucatan, who were near the point of hysteria, were concentrated in the city of Mérida, which the Mayas were surrounding. Most families moved downtown to gain some protection inside the city walls. O'Reilly offered Yucatan's annexation to the United States in exchange for help, but luckily for Mexico, political intrigues and rivalries in the US prevented the factions from reaching an agreement. The governor also offered the peninsula to Spain.

When Mérida was surrounded, the governor tried to order an evacuation, but he couldn't find paper in his office to print the proclamation.

Rumors ran through the streets that savages were everywhere. People escaped to the sea from [the port of] Sisal, Campeche or any other port where they could grab anything that floated, to take them anywhere. In the streets of Mérida and Campeche there was talk of general slaughter, elimination of the white population of Yucatan, which meant more than 140 thousand people, counting the mestizos.

But when the apocalypse was imminent, the terrified whites saw a miracle happen: the Maya suddenly left the site. A cloud of insects had appeared, winged ants, which for the Mayas announced the beginning of rains, meaning it was time to return to their crops. Years later, the son of one of the leaders explained:

It was scorching heat. Suddenly there appeared the winged ants in great clouds from the north, south, east and west, all over the place. When they saw this, those with my father said to each other, and said to their brothers, "The time has come for us to do our plantation, because if we do not do it, we will not have the Grace of God to fill our children´s belly." Thus they said and argued, and thought a lot, and when the morning came, my father's men said each one: "I'm leaving." And despite the pleas and threats of the bosses, each man rolled up his blanket and prepared his food bag, tightened the straps of his sandals and set off toward his house and his cornfield. Then the Batabob, knowing that it was useless to attack the city with the few remaining men, met in council and decided to go back home.

Mérida was saved for the time being, but the rebellion did not end. The Mayas, who had adopted the name of *Cruzoob* or "Crusaders," retreated south into the jungles and proclaimed the independent republic of Santa Cruz, which was recognized by Great Britain. For a very short time, there was a true Mayan nation in the 19th century, located in the extreme south of Mexico (in the modern state of Quintana Roo), resisting the constant siege of the government. That was until a new and terrible weapon arrived, the multi-shot rifle or machine gun, which caused horror among the Maya. It was hard to avoid a single shot charging with their machetes, but to throw themselves at the new machine guns was suicide. The Mayan chiefs of the different regions met in the city of Chan Santa Cruz, and after checking the lack of gunpowder, ammunition, and corn, they decided to set fire to the town and disperse in small groups. They entered the jungle and promised to meet again every full moon. In this way, under the presidency of Porfirio Díaz, the long resistance of the Maya came to an end in 1901. And thus ended the last great indigenous rebellion on the American continent.

Chapter 8 – The Mexican Revolution

In 1910, Porfirio Díaz was eighty years old and a relic. He had been born when California and Texas were still a part of Mexico. He had fought in the famous battle of Cinco de Mayo to stop the French and the monarchy. Most people in the country did not remember any other president than Díaz. Mexico enjoyed the Porfirian peace that was already being compared by some skeptics to the peace of the graveyards. He had been reelected six times, and although to a foreign observer, there was no need for social change since business was flourishing in Mexico, there was clear economic, political, and social unrest throughout the nation. Ninety percent of the country's inhabitants lived in poverty, and more than three-quarters of the population was indigenous. According to the country's ruling class, they were a burden, an ignorant and lazy mass, who were meant to be oppressed, subjugated, and exploited to death under the sun. "We were tough," admitted Díaz at the end of his era. "The poor are so ignorant that they have no power. We were tough. Sometimes to the point of being cruel. But all this was necessary for the life and progress of the nation."

Mexico entered the 20th century amidst workers' agitation. In the last years of Díaz's long tenure, the laborers began to rebel and were harshly repressed. Don Porfirio, as he was and is still called, always resolved in favor of foreign interests; for him, it was vital to maintain peace and order and preserve the confidence of international investors. But in 1908, the old dictator gave an interview to a North American journalist named James Creelman, where he finally conceded that he had had enough and that he would welcome the emergence of an opposition party. "I will welcome an opposition party. If it appears, I will see it as a blessing and not as an evil, and if it can develop power, not to exploit but to rule, I will stand by it, support it, advise it and forget myself in the successful inauguration of complete democratic government in the country." The interview provoked a hornet's nest. A son of a landowner with democratic ideals named Francisco Ignacio Madero began to campaign against Díaz, organizing a political party and touring the country. When Díaz sent him to jail and had himself reelected for the seventh time in the 1910 election, Madero realized that an armed revolution was the only way to democracy. He issued the Plan of San Luis, which called on all Mexicans to rise up against the dictatorship on November 20th, 1910.

The Mexican Revolution

The Mexican Revolution, which ran from 1910 to 1920, began as a democratic movement to oust President Díaz but ended up as a socialist revolution. At the same time, on the other side of the world, Vladimir Lenin called on the Russians to create a utopia controlled by the workers. Madero's call to arms did not generate much response among the middle, urban, and intellectual classes. But another sector, possibly the most exhausted, responded at first with some hesitation but then with unusual energy: the peasant class of northern and southern Mexico.

The world watched the Mexican Revolution with interest, and the movement grew uncontrollable. Two characters embody this important period better than anyone else. In the north, one of the most essential figures of the country's history appeared, Francisco "Pancho" Villa, who is known through many photographs as the archetype of the Mexican man: tall and stocky, wide hat, mustache, horse, gun in his hand, and a bullet-crossed chest. This northerner was driven by more than the democratic cause. He fought like a possessed man, holding hatred for the regime and against everything that reminded him of dictator Díaz, including the landowners and the rural guards who had harassed him for years. In one battle, Villa tricked the army by planting sticks with hats so that it would appear he had a larger force, which helped to instill panic among the enemy ranks. Besides his military genius, Villa had charisma: he gathered soldiers and volunteers from nothing, and people saw in him a symbol of their rage against a government that had forgotten the peasants. As such, legends began to be woven around him. He took Ciudad Juárez, a strategic point on the border with the United States, after two days of battle. US neighbors watched the clash from the other side, lying on the roof of train wagons to avoid loose bullets.

The other figure, almost a mirror of Villa, emerged at the other end of Mexico, in the southern mountains. He was tall, dark, and good-looking, with an even wider hat and a slightly old-fashioned mustache. Emiliano Zapata, a peasant leader, began to take the lands of the haciendas by force and distributed it among the people of Anenecuilco, his hometown. Zapata strengthened his legitimacy by rejecting bribes and the temptation of self-benefit. He once said, "Check the Colonial titles and take what is owed to the people." In a few months, he managed to gather an army of twelve thousand peasants. He entered Cuautla, his first major city, while his peasants carried banners of the Virgin of Guadalupe.

Both unique cases in Mexico's history, for so long a country of military men conspiring to seize power, neither Villa nor Zapata were interested in the presidency or any other political position, although they had the possibility of sitting on the chair. Pancho Villa openly acknowledged that he was an uneducated man and only wanted justice for the humble. Zapata said that the chair had the power to change people. "I'd rather not sit down," he said when he had it in front of him in the National Palace, "because when someone is good, and sits on this chair, when he gets up he's become bad." Madero won the election in what was perhaps the first democratic exercise in the history of Mexico, winning 99 percent of the popular vote, but he did not last long. As he was an idealist who could not control the magnitude of the forces he had unleashed, in 1913, he was in conflict with everyone—he could not decide to resolve once and for all the peasants' demands. Worst of all, he was surrounded by adversaries, with a vociferous press that took advantage of the same freedom he had given them. In February, he was killed in a tangled conspiracy, which the US ambassador had a lot to do with, that had been orchestrated by an old general named Victoriano Huerta. After appointing an interim president, who lasted in power a ridiculous 45 minutes—a record in history—General Huerta became Mexico's new dictator. His act enraged all the factions—Villa, Zapata, and the others—who united around a common goal: to overthrow the traitor who, with a bullet, had destroyed Mexico's opportunity to become a democratic country.

At the end of 1914, the powerful armies of Pancho Villa from the north—the famous "Dorados," which was followed by thousands of women to cook for them—and Emiliano Zapata from the south—mostly Native American peasants with white cotton pants—marched into Mexico City a few days apart. In December, the two popular leaders were photographed together in the National Palace around the presidential chair. Villa sat on it, laughing. It was a unique moment that has never been repeated. They themselves did not understand the true magnitude of what was happening. For the first time in Mexico's history, two popular armies had captured power. However, neither Villa nor Zapata knew what to do with it. They could have ordered anything, but neither of them had the intellectual capacity or desire to be president, and they were the first to admit it. They put a puppet president in the National Palace and let the historical opportunity pass. Soon, others would seize the void they had left. The Mexican Revolution was fragmented into many leaders fighting against one another. Zapata returned to his southern mountains, and Villa lost a disastrous battle in Celaya. His powerful northern division never recovered from the blow and fragmented. At the end of 1916, Pancho Villa was isolated in the north with just a few faithful men, being hunted as a vulgar bandit, when he decided to attack the United States.

It was not a large-scale invasion. Villa was with no more than four hundred men, but it is the only time to date that the continental United States has been invaded by an army with their boots on the ground. Around four o'clock in the morning, Villa burst into the town of Columbus, New Mexico, as the people slept peacefully. The Villistas attacked from four directions, aiming everywhere, looting, and unleashing chaos. The inhabitants woke up terrified. From afar, people could see the glow of farms and houses engulfed in flames, and they could hear the wild cries of the Villistas, who had seized about one hundred horses as well as ammunition.

In the United States, many outraged and opportunistic voices called for a new intervention to punish Mexico, but with World War I going on in Europe, President Woodrow Wilson knew that the path of prudence was best. However, he still sent an expedition under the command of General John J. Pershing and ten thousand men to capture Villa. "Where is Pancho Villa?" Pershing asked in his broken Spanish in each ranch and village in the mountains. "He went that way, to the next town uphill," the women answered, covering half their faces with a rebozo. When the next hamlet appeared, the men on horseback loaded their rifles and blocked the escape routes. "Is Pancho Villa here?" Pershing roared. "Villa has just left, *señor.* If you go that way, you will surely reach him in half an hour," the locals responded, pointing toward the opposite side. "I have the honor of informing you," Pershing wrote his report at the end of the day, "that

Francisco Villa is everywhere and nowhere." The punitive expedition returned to the United States without fulfilling its objective.

In private, the famous military general later admitted that "when the true history is written, it will not be a very inspiring chapter for school children, or even grownups to contemplate. Having dashed into Mexico with the intention of eating the Mexicans raw, we turned back at the first repulse and are now sneaking home under cover, like a whipped cur with its tail between its legs."

The Zimmermann Telegram

During the Mexican Revolution, Mexico became involved in an incident that changed the course of world history. In 1917, in the middle of World War I, Germany launched an ambitious plan. The United States took notice when the British intelligence service intercepted a telegram sent by German Foreign Secretary Arthur Zimmermann to the German ambassador in Mexico, Heinrich von Eckardt. When the British showed the paper to the US embassy in London, the Americans thought it was a joke. But once they learned it was authentic, and its content was disseminated in the American press, the American people burned with indignation. In the telegram, Arthur Zimmermann instructed the ambassador to begin negotiations with the president of Mexico, Venustiano Carranza, so that, with German support, Mexico could declare war on the US. In return, it would get "generous financial support," and if the Central Powers won World War I, Mexico would recover the states of Texas, New Mexico, and Arizona, the territories that were lost in 1847. The telegram, decoded by the intelligence of Great Britain, said:

We intend to begin on the first of February unrestricted submarine warfare. We shall endeavor in spite of this to keep the United States of America neutral. In the event of this not succeeding, we make Mexico a proposal of alliance on the following basis: make war together, make peace together, generous financial support and an understanding on our part that Mexico is to reconquer the lost territory in Texas, New Mexico, and Arizona. The settlement in detail is left to you. You will inform the President of the above most secretly as soon as the outbreak of war with the United States of America is certain, and add the suggestion that he should, on his own initiative, invite Japan to immediate adherence and at the same time mediate between Japan and ourselves. Please call the President's attention to the fact that the ruthless employment of our submarines now offers the prospect of compelling England in a few months to make peace. Signed, ZIMMERMANN.

Although the telegram did not actually reach Carranza, the Mexican president sent his foreign minister to talk with Heinrich von Eckardt, who had been sent from Berlin. Carranza also established a commission to investigate whether Mexico should agree to the terms of the telegram. The Germans promised money and weapons to help wage war on the United States, but most likely, Carranza was not taking the Germans seriously, and he was just trying to get funds from whatever source in order to consolidate his power with minimal commitment. On April 14th, 1917, Carranza formally declined Zimmermann's proposal, but he did not close all the doors. "If Mexico is dragged into the [First] World War in spite of everything, we'll see. For now the alliance has been frustrated, but it will be necessary later on at a certain moment." The Zimmermann Telegram threw the hitherto neutral United States into the First World War. The telegram's plan went nowhere, but its content again aroused suspicions against the southern neighbor of the US, and the remembrance of the territories lost in 1847 once more removed consciences on both sides of the border.

In 1919, Carranza was firmly in power. The United States had recognized his government, and his main enemies had vanished. Villa remained hidden in the northern mountains, protected by the local population. After a decade and a million deaths (7 percent of the population but a much higher percentage of the economically active population), the Mexican Revolution, which was initially started to restore democracy and then to regenerate the country's economic system, proved to be the most expensive war, in terms of both money and human lives, in Mexico's history. But the long struggle did raise awareness of the need for social justice, starting with land distribution and education for the common people. The ideals promoted by fighters such as Madero, Villa, and especially Zapata were embodied in a new constitution promulgated in 1917, which still governs the land today.

The Mexican Revolution of 1910, a decisive event in the formation of 20th-century Mexico's philosophy, economy, and even artistic development, brought the rise of middle and popular classes and the displacement of the oligarchy that had run the show throughout almost all of the 19th century. In its first stage, the revolution was initiated by just another elite, but the popular classes took it from their hands. From 1913 on, the middle class assumed the leadership, and the peasant classes were positioned for the first time as a formidable political force with a voice and vote in the country's development. The new state, born in 1920 when the bullets stopped flying and the dust settled, was not democratic, but it was indeed nationalist and popular. It spawned authoritarian leaders, but they were men forged in the Mexican Revolution, and so, they had a social conscience and willingness to carry out a comprehensive agrarian reform and the organization of the working class. Finally, a stable state was born, with great popular support and with the reluctant acceptance of the United States.

It was the surviving revolutionaries and the followers of those who had begun the great social departure—Zapata, Madero, Carranza, and Villa, who were all killed by their enemies—who created the new Mexican identity. After a hundred years of calamities, the country seemed to have found a route that could accommodate everyone. The revolutionaries integrated the whole country into a new nationalist state that was not xenophobic; it was revolutionary but with stable institutions.

It fell on the great Mexican artists from the 1920s onward—painters Diego Rivera, Frida Kahlo, and José Clemente Orozco; writers Juan Rulfo and Octavio Paz; musicians Manuel M. Ponce, Carlos Chávez, and José Pablo Moncayo—to show what Mexicanity means. Thanks to them, and others of their generation, Mexico began to be recognized as a country full of people with cultural expressions on par with the rest of the world.

Chapter 9 – The Cristeros

"The Church has exceeded our wildest hopes in decreeing the suspension of religious services; nothing could be more pleasing to us. We have got the clergy by the throat and will do everything to strangle it."

—Mexican Minister of Interior, Adalberto Tejeda, 1926

The Mexican Revolution produced the Constitution of 1917 and a political class that abhorred the Catholic Church, which was, nonetheless, still the predominant religion of the country. During the war years, it was a common spectacle to see generals and leaders humiliating priests and seizing and plundering churches, which they would adapt as public offices or seats of state congresses or simply just tear down. The government's anti-religiousness climaxed with President Plutarco Elías Calles, a general with open communist sympathies.

With no counterweights, the state that emerged from the Mexican Revolution tried to put religious institutions under dictatorial control. This produced one of the most little-known episodes in the history of Mexico, one that, for many years, the state tried to slide under the rug: the Cristero War, a kind of counter-revolution that the new state never suspected could happen. The Cristero War, also known as La

Cristiada, ravaged the whole center of the country. The Constitution of 1917 restricted religious education, outlawed monastic orders, banned worship outside churches, and turned church property over to the ownership of the state. Further legal measures by the Calles administration gave the government the authority to determine the number of clergy officials in each state and prohibited religious publications, priestly celibacy, and monastic life, among other harsh measures. In those days, government forces stormed many churches on the pretext that they were not fulfilling the law, and they expelled nuns, priests, and bishops from the country. In some states, such as Tabasco, the governors forced the priests to marry.

When the Church responded with the announcement that it would suspend worship as a protest, Calles was pleased because he was sure that the measure would ultimately destroy the Catholic Church. At the same time, the most anticlerical president ever became active in religion; however, it was not Catholicism. Calles supported a schismatic movement to create a Mexican Catholic Apostolic Church, whose head was a rebel bishop named Joaquín Pérez. The proposed Church would not depend on the Vatican, and its highest authority would be Joaquín "the Patriarch" Pérez.

Calles also responded to the strike of public worship with the banning of private worship; this unprecedented measure, reminiscent of Christian persecution in ancient times, effectively made religion illegal. Thousands of people went to churches to receive the sacrament that, in a matter of days, would be grounds for imprisonment. Thousands of children were baptized, Masses were celebrated continuously for days, and an archbishop fainted from exhaustion after confirming five thousand people in a single day. The so-called Calles Law came in full force on August 1ˢᵗ, 1926, and the government sent its forces to seal the doors of the churches and seize their inventories, and then closed confessional schools, as well as convents and monasteries. Many Catholics protested. The government responded by imprisoning more priests. In 1927, Father

Francisco Vera was arrested for celebrating Mass and taken to the firing squad. The general who ordered the execution of Father Vera, who stood in his full attire with hands clasped in a sign of prayer before the four-men firing squad, took an infamous photo of the execution and sent it to President Calles, who, in turn, passed it to the press. Dismissed by intellectuals and the state as a reactionary movement to the progressive Mexican Revolution, the Cristero War had indeed been spawned by a genuine and bloody religious persecution.

Mexicans to this day remember tales told by their grandparents about families hiding priests and nuns in their attics and cellars for years to save them from arrest, deportation, or execution by firing squad. The religious war lasted from 1926 to 1929. Catholic peasants of the states of Guanajuato, Zacatecas, Aguascalientes, Jalisco, and Colima formed resistance groups with no experience, especially compared to the 70,000-men federal army, fresh from the Mexican Revolution. The Cristeros rode in groups of fifty to one hundred men, fighting local wars completely unprepared, only to be massacred. But things soon changed.

It was during the Cristero War that the government first used aviation for military purposes, even bombarding the famous sculpture of Christ the King in Guanajuato. In a year, however, the Cristero forces reached twenty thousand combatants. Women played an important role in the war. While in the Mexican Revolution, their role had been to cook for the troops, during the Cristiada, they served as spies, propagandists, logistics, and resistance. When the army was going to seize a church, women usually occupied it while the men defended the surroundings. In 1927, the women also entered into combat when the Joan of Arc Brigade was established, named after the maid of Orléans, France, who had just been canonized in Rome. The Joan of Arc Brigade consisted of 650 women who, although they did not take up arms, did war work. They had ranks of general, colonel, and captain, and they controlled ammunition, weapons, medical assistance, and did espionage work. The brigade was composed mostly of teenage women carrying weapons and ammunition to the battlefields, putting their lives at risk.

In the beginning, the Cristero movement suffered from the lack of a leading figure or central command until Enrique Gorostieta, a soldier who had fought in the Mexican Revolution, emerged and brought organization and unity to an effort that was local and split up. The movement that the government initially criticized and derided as a phony revolution now deserved not only their concern but also the Vatican's and the rest of the world. The Cristeros were never a real threat to the government, as they could not aspire to overthrow the regime. This was a movement located in central Mexico, and the men had no military training and many internal divisions. And they certainly did not have the support of the Church or the Vatican, at least officially.

In 1928, General Álvaro Obregón was reelected to the presidency. When he was celebrating his victory in a restaurant with friends and allies, a young Catholic man posing as a cartoonist approached and asked him if he could draw a portrait. President-elect Obregón agreed, saw the cartoon and, laughing, passed it among those present. Then the young man pulled out a gun and emptied his gun with six shots. The officers tried to execute him right there, but a person stopped them, saying that it was necessary to know who had sent him. The young man was a religious fanatic who, in his statement, said he had done it "so that Christ our Lord can reign in Mexico." The Church condemned the killing, and the murderer was executed by a firing squad in 1929. Before he was shot, he extended his arms to form the cross and died without being able to say, like all the Cristeros during the war, "Long live Christ the King." José de León Toral, the confessed assassin, became a martyr for some Cristeros.

The movement, crossed out as a fabricated reactionary movement by the revolutionary generation of 1910, became important enough to alarm global public opinion and to pressure the government and the

Church to reach an agreement. In 1928, Pope Pius XI sent a letter to Mexican Catholics asking them to have trust, as negotiations were ongoing. In 1929, when the Cristero forces had already reached fifty thousand people, and countless combatants and priests lay in their graves, representatives of the Vatican met with the Mexican clergy and the United States ambassador, Dwight W. Morrow. President Calles, in the last year of his tenure, also met with representatives of the Mexican and international Church, as well as Ambassador Morrow, to try to attain a solution. In June, the government and the Church signed a peace agreement, and an unspoken promise was reached not to apply the anticlerical laws. The Mexican Church resumed worship in the Basilica of Guadalupe, under the image that was believed to be miraculous since the colonial period, the image that had mobilized Mexicans at different times to rebel against injustice. The Cristero combatants, who were required to present themselves in order to deliver their weapons and receive safe passage, disbanded and vanished as they had come, without notifying anyone, and returned to their ranches and towns in central Mexico. The women renovated many ruined churches, confident that their holy war had come to an end.

The relations between the Church and the state would remain tense for the rest of the century. In the next decade, the same circumstances recurred, and a second and shorter Cristiada swept the central part of the country. As the 1940s entered, President Manuel Ávila Camacho apparently settled the matter when he declared that he was a Catholic. When Ávila said, "I am a believer," he was the first Mexican president since the Mexican Revolution to openly admit it. But the world was going to take a turn with World War II, and Mexico's priorities, like those of the rest of the world, would change radically. Unlike the First World War, this time Mexico would need to make a decision that would define its future forever. Would it side with the Allies or with the Axis?

Chapter 10 – The Second World War and the Mexican Miracle

Lázaro Cárdenas, perhaps the most popular and respected president in Mexico's history, came to the presidency with a pacified country, but the countryside was ruined, and the peasant class was still waiting for the promises of the Mexican Revolution, land and freedom, to be fulfilled. Cárdenas carried out an agrarian reform as Zapata would have wanted, under which a total of eighteen million hectares would be distributed to the peasant communities under a property regime called *ejido*, which prevented the lands from being sold, bought, disposed of, or lost to debtors. Cárdenas also nationalized the oil industry at a critical time; it was 1938, a year before the beginning of the Second World War. At this time, the country had become a budding oil power, and its main clients, Great Britain and the United States, owned the facilities nationalized by the government. Upon hearing the news, they promoted an economic boycott to starve Mexico, and a few investors in those nations even called for a new intervention to compensate for the losses. But the beginning of World War II changed the whole scenario.

The Western powers were alarmed to see that Nazi Germany had not joined the boycott against Mexico. On the contrary, the Third

Reich sold Mexico the necessary chemicals to keep its oil industry running so they could sell the essential fuel to Führer Adolf Hitler. With the Anglo-Saxon embargo, Nazi Germany became the main buyer of Mexican oil. Britain and the United States realized that their small revenge had thrown Mexico into the Nazi sphere. Mexico passed from selling one million barrels of oil a year to the Third Reich to almost five million in 1939, the year of the invasion of Poland. It is entirely possible some blitzkrieg tanks that crushed the Polish villages were fueled by Mexican oil. Nazi Germany began to send spies and conspirators to Mexico, who carried out the essential task of sending sensitive information back about the United States while initiating an ideological struggle to cast all of Latin America to the Axis side. But Mexico kept a sound and clear-minded policy. When Hitler annexed Austria in 1938, beginning his expansionist policy that no one dared to criticize, Mexico was the only country in the world to protest against the *Anschluss.*

President Cárdenas got a secret report sent by his Ministry of Interior, officially informing him that there was a powerful Nazi network operating in the country. Until the end of his time in office, Cárdenas maintained his pro-democratic discourse but also neutrality in the war, as well as commercial ties with both sides.

By the end of 1940, with a presidential election approaching, the Nazi intervention in Mexico became intolerable for the United States, and it began to press Cárdenas. In 1941, the new president, Manuel Ávila Camacho, signed an agreement with the United States allowing it to use its air bases and supported a commercial treaty to sell oil again. This decision cost Mexico. In May of 1942, Germany bombed and sank several Mexican ships in the Gulf of Mexico in retaliation for selling fuel to the führer's enemy.

The first ship was *Potrero del Llano.* The boat was carrying 6,000 tons of oil and 35 crew members. Thirteen perished, including its captain, while the rest were rescued by an American ship. Some newspapers in Mexico reported that the Germans had exterminated the survivors struggling to stay afloat with submachine guns. The arrival of the corpses to Mexican territory deeply impacted the national mood, and more people were inclined to Mexico breaking its neutrality. In the following days, German submarines attacked more crafts. Finally, on May 28th, Mexico declared "a state of war" with the Axis powers. Although Mexico was the heir to a long tradition of bad American ambassadors, on that occasion, it got a shrewd visionary and an attentive ambassador who was concerned for the future of Mexico. George Messersmith saw the convenience not only of Mexico declaring war and supporting the US with raw materials and men to harvest their fields but also its ability to send a combat force to the war front. It would be the first time in the country's history. To achieve this, Messersmith was going to have to pass through a maze of interests, opposition, and bureaucracy.

For the Mexicans themselves, it was a surprise to learn that this time their country was on the same side as the United States. There was still much resentment one hundred years after the war and the loss of its northern territory. The Mexican-American historian and writer for *The New York Times* Anita Brenner told how the news was received in the town of San Andrés. People were enjoying the evening on the plaza benches when the radio announced that Mexico was at war yet again. The people shouted, "*Viva México!* Death to the *gringos!*" (*gringos* referring to the Americans) and even "*Viva la Revolución!*" Suddenly, the town's telegrapher interrupted the jubilant exclamations. "Idiots! Imbeciles!" he said. "We're against Germany! ... Don't you understand the Americans are on our side? We´re fighting Fascism!" On the other side of the crowd, where the women were, an old, cracked voice cried, "God preserve us! Who would have ever told me that I would come to be praying for *gringos...!*"

The Aztec Eagles

Thanks to the work of Ambassador Messersmith in Mexico and the US, both presidents agreed on the convenience of Mexico participating, albeit symbolically, with an infantry division or an air combat squad. Ávila Camacho and Franklin D. Roosevelt agreed that it would be best to send a squad of fighter planes to General Douglas MacArthur, who was in the Pacific at the time. Air squadrons presented fewer human casualties and had a superior destruction capacity. The fighter squadrons also constituted the first line of attack to destroy military targets, force the enemy to flee, and clear the way for ground troops. Despite their small size in comparison with units fighting on the ground, the thirty-pilot squadrons were a significant factor on the Pacific front, which was ultimately the last stage of the Second World War. In 1944, Mexico finally sent their group of thirty pilots for training in the United States to fight against Japan in the liberation of the Philippines. The men of the 201ˢᵗ Fighter Squadron, also known as the Aztec Eagles, arrived in Manila in the nick of time on April 30ᵗʰ, 1945, as the war was coming to a close.

At first, when they arrived at the air base near Manila, the Mexicans received cold and even hostile treatment from the Americans, who felt that the "petite" pilots—as they were much shorter than the Marines—were only going to get in the way. Before going into combat, spirits were heated and near fistfights. It was just the tension before the action. The Aztec Eagles finally received the order to board their planes in May 1945 and receive their baptism of fire. Before doing so, they wrote letters home. Although we now know that the Second World War would last less than four more months, at the time, the Allies were looking forward to a prolonged and costly war in terms of human lives, as Japan had sworn it would never surrender.

Back home in Mexico, an excited and nervous press reported that the Mexicans had just entered into combat in the Philippines against Japanese units. Twenty aircraft from the 201ˢᵗ Squadron, under the orders of Captain Radamés Gaxiola, took part in the operation, bombing and gunning tanks and trucks on the island of Luzon. The Japanese responded with anti-aircraft fire. The first casualty came in June when 22-year-old pilot Fausto Vega Santander died during a difficult mission against a Japanese ammunition depot. In addition to anti-aircraft fire, the Japanese had three natural defenses in the form of high cliffs; the only possible approach was from the sea and through a narrow opening. The 201ˢᵗ Squadron's commander suggested that the only way to destroy the depot was to dive-bomb it from a very high altitude, which was virtually a suicide mission. The Mexicans succeeded where other Allied pilots had failed, but the act also cost Mexico its first pilot overseas.

The 201ˢᵗ Squadron accumulated 785 defensive missions and six offensive missions in the Philippines and Taiwan, and it is calculated that they eliminated, nullified, or expelled around thirty thousand Japanese soldiers over two months. But Mexico's role in World War II was more symbolic than real. Mexico only lost five pilots, which is a footnote compared to the over 400,000 American or the almost nine million Russian casualties. The 201ˢᵗ Squadron's greatest triumph was not achieved in the airspace of the Far East but in the diplomatic realm. Thanks to its participation, a new era of international relations began between Mexico and the United States, two countries that had been hostile and distrustful toward each other since basically forever. It also allowed the former to be on the side of the winners in the Second World War, and it became a founding member of the United Nations.

The Northward Migration

The Second World War brought a demographic phenomenon that helps to explain present-day Mexico: the migration of peasants and unskilled workers to the United States. Since the Mexican Revolution, some Mexicans had emigrated north to escape violence. The Great Depression of the 1930s saw the mass deportation of Mexicans, including those families who had lived on the north side of the Rio Grande since before the war with the United States, the so-called Chicanos. But the migration northward in large numbers began in the 1940s. Contrary to what many believe, it was the United States who first asked Mexico to send workers to harvest its fields because hands and arms were lacking for agriculture. In 1942, in the first harvest after the attack on Pearl Harbor, California farmers expressed their concern to the government that there would be a shortage of workers in the fields and requested that their government import one hundred thousand Mexican workers.

The governments, represented by Franklin D. Roosevelt and Manuel Ávila Camacho, signed an urgent agreement known as the Bracero Program, *bracero* being a Spanish word meaning a man who works with his arms. The program was given a limited duration and would last only during the war years. Mexico even had the luxury of establishing conditions in order to send its peasants: migrants would get roundtrip transportation from their towns to the harvest fields, they would be paid the same wage as the Americans who did the same work, and they would receive protection and essential healthcare. In the first year of the Bracero Program, four thousand Mexican workers entered the United States with all benefits. Only one year later, the number increased to 44,000 and then 62,000 in the last year of World War II. The program was too favorable for the business of US farmers, who demanded that the binational agreement continue for a few more years. The Bracero Program came to legally admit up to 200,000 workers per year in the 1950s, not counting those who were attracted to agricultural companies outside the institutional channels; those workers received lower salaries. In 1956, the number of temporary and legal agricultural workers in the United States reached a record high of 450,000 people. American agricultural workers had the possibility to leave their jobs in the countryside to go look for urban jobs, which, in turn, led to greater demand for agricultural workers and greater migration of Mexican peasants. The flow continued for many years with the tacit approval of the US government and with poor conditions for Mexicans. In this way, a migration process from south to north started, and it continues today.

This demographic movement was also the origin of two developments that characterized the second half of the 20th century: the expansion of Mexican culture in the United States, mainly in

Texas, California, and New Mexico; and the Chicano movement in the southern United States, where the figure of César Chávez, the son of poor Mexican migrants, is paramount. A former worker in the vineyards in California, Chávez fought for the dignification of Hispanic American farmworkers. Inspired by Gandhi and his techniques of nonviolence, such as civil resistance and fasting, Chávez first encouraged agricultural workers of Mexican origin to organize, to register to vote, to voice complaints, and to strike.

Initially, Chávez began to unionize the fields and orchards of California, where he issued a call to boycott grapes from the state, and his movement acquired such a force that it captured worldwide attention. Agricultural entrepreneurs ended up recognizing the union founded by Chávez, United Farm Workers. At a time when the West saw communism as the worst of evils, Chávez was being monitored by the FBI. "It is my deepest belief that only by giving our lives do we find life," he said once. "I am convinced that the truest act of courage, the strongest act of manliness is to sacrifice ourselves for others in a totally non-violent struggle for justice." César Chávez thus represents the best of the Mexican diaspora. He became an icon of the Mexican community in the United States and indirectly, thanks to his work for the empowerment of Chicanos, also became a factor in the emergence of this ethnic group as an important electoral political force.

Chapter 11 – End of Century Pangs

"We Mexicans, on the other hand, fight against imaginary entities, vestiges of the past or ghosts engendered by ourselves. They are impalpable and invincible because they are not outside us but within us."

—Nobel Prize Winner Octavio Paz

Mexico lived its golden age— "the Mexican miracle" as it was known throughout the world—in the 1950s and 1960s. For the first time since it stopped calling itself New Spain, the country was at peace, with economic growth, social peace, a healthy demographic expansion that began to populate the farthest corners of the country, and flourishing arts. A new appreciation for its pre-Hispanic past, as well as the archaeological works in Mexico City to dig up the ruins of Tenochtitlan and restoring the Mayan pyramids and temples in Yucatan, made Mexico one of the main tourist destinations. Great personalities visited Mexico for the first time, such as Dwight D. Eisenhower, John F. Kennedy, Charles de Gaulle, Josip Broz Tito, Queen Juliana of the Netherlands, and Akihito and Michiko, the rulers of Japan from 1989 to 2019 (although it should be noted they visited Japan in the 1960s). The new Basilica of Guadalupe was inaugurated, and the National Museum of Anthropology was the object of general admiration. How had Mexico achieved this miracle?

Post-war Mexico had adopted a plan of nationalist development. Its economic strategy was to adopt a protectionist policy with high import tariffs in order to develop its own industry. The government encouraged national investments and offered clear rules and reliability to investors. At the same time, a welfare state was created that offered workers free education, free healthcare, price controls, and the right to organize in exchange for discipline and loyalty to the post-revolutionary regime. This stage was known as "stabilizing development," and it allowed Mexican baby boomers to enjoy a period of unprecedented prosperity and stability. Economic growth was historic, reaching a yearly 6.8 percent on average. Industrial production also grew at a similar pace, and best of all, all of this was achieved without inflation. On the other hand, in a more subtle way, the government quickly and effectively suppressed any alteration of order.

But in the late 1960s, the model began to show its limitations. In 1968, when student protests broke out all over the world, and the press talked about the riots in Paris, the Mexican counterculture also aired its demands, and the students took the streets. Again, the student protests focused on the capital, and they quickly increased until they became alarming for the government. The pro-government press—practically all the newspapers—talked about a communist conspiracy.

A few days before the 1968 Summer Olympics were held in Mexico City, the government did the unthinkable. On October 2nd, dozens of tanks and five thousand soldiers stormed from all sides on a student demonstration that was protesting peacefully in the Tlatelolco Square and fired on approximately ten thousand students and others who attended the rally. The crowd panicked and started running over dead bodies. The assault on Tlatelolco left a death toll that has never been established since the government took care to buy the press, seize all photographic materials, and hide the dead. During the night, the fire department showered Tlatelolco Square with fire hoses to rinse the blood. Eyewitnesses and survivors estimate that up to five hundred people died that day.

The Tlatelolco massacre was not an isolated event. It was the climax of a series of protests and the manifestation of a visible malaise: the stabilizing development, with all its merits, had developed Mexico, but it had burnt out. The channels of participation in politics were closed, and although elections were held, democracy was fictitious, and the gap between rich and poor had widened. The student massacre was the drop that spilled the glass and the clearest sign that the long post-revolutionary state—represented by the state party, the Institutional Revolutionary Party (PRI)—had become a kind of "perfect dictatorship." Many of the disappointed and angry leaders of the student protests went underground, and during the next two decades, clandestine guerrilla movements surfaced in northern and southern Mexico. The government was implacable and adopted dirty war tactics against the most visible guerrilla factions. At the same time, the wealthy farmers in the south formed government-sponsored paramilitary groups to suppress any indigenous resistance. More slowly and discreetly, another movement was gradually maturing, which would make its appearance two decades later.

The government tried to make a left turn toward a welfare state to help fix the acute social lags, and it laid the foundations for a new development model supported by a large treasure that had been literally hidden underground: its immense oil reserves. At the beginning of the 1980s, Mexico was one of the largest oil producers in the world. It had such an influence in the market that it constituted a power similar to that of OPEC. But the temporary bonanza came with an expensive bill. The price of oil suddenly collapsed from 125 dollars per barrel in 1980 to 64 dollars in 1985. For a country like Mexico, which had borrowed extensively to develop its oil industry and tied its economy to the so-called "black gold," the price drop could only mean problems. The 1980s was the "lost decade," not only for Mexico but for Latin America. Mexico renegotiated its foreign debt and adopted a more open and liberal economic model based not only on oil exports but on a more diversified industry and foreign trade. President Carlos Salinas de Gortari, a reformer, signed a free trade agreement with the United States and Canada, raising the question among international analysts whether North America would become an economic bloc in the style of the European Union. But it was too late. A voice from the past, which emerged from the southern mountains, reminded the world that the indigenous cause was far from being resolved.

The Zapatistas

Seventy-five years after the death of Emiliano Zapata, the idolized peasant freedom fighter of 1910, the indigenous people of the south declared war on the Mexican government, claiming Zapata's legacy. The indigenous armies with obsolete weapons and their faces covered with handkerchiefs took the town of San Cristóbal de las Casas on January 1ˢᵗ, 1994, the same day the North American Free Trade Agreement (NAFTA) went into effect. In the early hours, they released indigenous prisoners and destroyed land titles. The decision to begin their rebellion in San Cristóbal was a fine irony: as recently as the decade of the 1950s, Native Americans were not allowed to enter the city, which was a picturesque tourist destination. The date chosen was also a blunt message. While the government looked outside, pretending to be a first-world country with the signing of NAFTA, the Zapatista Army of National Liberation was a reminder that the Native Americans in Mexico were still there. On January 1ˢᵗ, the Zapatista forces, which were formed by fighters of the Tzotzil, Tzeltal, Tojolab'al, and Ch'ol ethnic groups, took the other six villages in the San Cristóbal region with rifles, machetes, and knives. They wore brown shirts, green pants, and rubber boots. Some brought backpacks and sophisticated firearms, while others carried wooden rifles painted with shoe grease.

In a statement that surprised the world, the Zapatistas announced their intention to march to Mexico City to defeat the federal army and liberate cities. They accused all of the previous governments of practicing an undeclared genocidal war against indigenous peoples, without caring that they were "starving and dying of curable diseases, not caring that we have nothing, absolutely nothing, not a decent roof, no land, no work, no health, no food, no education." At the head of the uprising was an anonymous character with a pipe and a ski mask, Rafael Sebastián Guillén Vicente, although his eyes did not look indigenous. His attire was completed by a bandolier crossing his chest, a submachine gun, a small pipe in his mouth, and a way of communicating that demonstrated high education. Guillén, better known as Subcomandante Marcos, had lived for decades in the mountains of Mexico, organizing the rebellion. "Forgive the inconvenience," the Zapatista leader told an angry tour guide who complained that he had to take his group to the ruins of Palenque, "but this is a revolution."

Marcos was not exaggerating in his statement. Half of the indigenous population of Chiapas, which was rich in natural resources but the second poorest state in the republic, had no income at all. The natives, who had once populated the entire territory, had been withdrawing toward the south over the last five centuries. The mountainous terrain of Chiapas, which was difficult to exploit and traverse, accommodated most of the country's indigenous peoples. The Zapatistas, of which approximately one-third were armed indigenous women, were poor, low in number —having approximately three thousand troops—and clearly did not pose a risk to the government, but President Carlos Salinas, nevertheless, decided to respond brutally. Firstly, the government sowed the idea that the Zapatistas were foreign guerrillas, terrorists, or drug traffickers, but they weren't actually any of those.

A column of eight hundred soldiers arrived in the town of Ocosingo in the afternoon of January 2nd, 1994. Ocosingo is a town in the mountains with twelve thousand inhabitants near the border of Guatemala. The Zapatistas had pulled out of most of the towns after the arrival of the army but not Ocosingo. They were concentrated in the market, where a battle ensued that lasted all night. On January 3rd, the army decided to take the market by storm. With instructions from the higher command to have no second thoughts about summary executions, the federal troops raided the city center. Later, the fight continued house by house. At night, the Zapatistas tried to break the siege by concentrating their forces on a single point and tried to reach a hill that would take them back to the jungle, but they were unprepared. The Ocosingo massacre reverberated worldwide. To recover other towns that could not be seized by ground forces, the president approved the use of the Mexican Air Force. Photographs of indigenous men and women killed in their own lands traveled the world, despite the army's efforts to clear the battlefield, and it had a shattering media effect against the Mexican government. The images are chilling, as if they were taken from a barbaric past. The confrontations continued for twelve days and ended when the government recovered the occupied towns, with hundreds of Zapatistas dead. The indigenous peoples were driven back to the jungle of Chiapas, and President Carlos Salinas assured the nation that the government was in control.

However, Salinas had made a terrible miscalculation. The images of the brief war against the native peoples impacted large sectors of Mexican society. Ten days after the start of the conflict, more than one hundred thousand people demonstrated in Mexico City in support of the Zapatistas. The president flinched. The Native Americans had awakened, once again, international consciousness and shaken Mexican society. The just nature of their demands called worldwide attention. Soon, thousands of international observers arrived. In a matter of weeks, the Zapatista rebellion was one of the most famous social movements in the world and had awakened an unexpected level of solidarity. "We did not go to war on January 1 to kill, or to have them kill us. We went to make ourselves heard," said Marcos, and he had accomplished just that.

The Mexican government was the first to be surprised by the uprising and the degree of attention it gained internationally, especially the figure of the enigmatic Subcomandante Marcos, who became a celebrity among intellectuals around the world. A ceasefire was declared, and a pardon was offered by the government. "What are they going to pardon us for?" the hooded leader asked in a new statement. "For not dying of hunger? For not accepting our misery in silence? For not humbly accepting the huge historic burden of disdain and abandonment? For having risen up in arms when we found all other paths closed? For having shown the country and the whole world that human dignity still exists and is in the hearts of the most impoverished inhabitants? For having made careful preparations before beginning our fight? For having brought guns to battle instead of bows and arrows? For being mostly Indigenous? Who should ask for forgiveness and who can grant it? Those who, for years and years, sat before a full table and satiated themselves while we sat with death, as such a daily factor in our lives that we stopped even fearing it?"

Soon, the peace negotiations began. The bishop of San Cristóbal, Samuel Ruiz, a respected figure that the rebels trusted and a priest identified with liberation theology, acted as a mediator. The Zapatistas demanded a new relationship between the state and the indigenous peoples. The San Andrés Accords proposed the right to autonomy of the indigenous peoples, meaning they would decide how to organize themselves politically, socially, economically, and culturally. They asked the state to set up mechanisms to guarantee conditions that would allow them to satisfactorily accomplish their nourishment, health, and housing. In their view, Mexico's policy for Native Americans should set up priority programs for the improvement of health and nourishment of children, as well as programs for the training of women. The administration of the new president, Ernesto Zedillo, could accept these social demands, but the heart of the San

Andrés Accords—autonomy—was too much for a government that perhaps feared losing Chiapas, as it had already once happened in the 19th century. This would have been the first step toward Mexico's "balkanization," a concern no doubt inferred from the Yugoslav Wars, which at that time was at its peak.

In February 1995, the government made a surprise counterattack, violating the conditions of the ceasefire. The government also disclosed the identity of Subcomandante Marcos, who was a former student of philosophy at Mexico City's UNAM (National Autonomous University of Mexico), and recovered the Zapatista territory by force. In the early hours of February 9th, the army broke the Native American positions with planes, helicopters, and soldiers on foot, demolishing houses, killing farm animals, and destroying crops. The inhabitants, fearing reprisals, left the villages and took refuge in the mountains, including children. Zedillo delivered a triumphal address on national television, but the government strategy failed again. By showing Marcos's face on television without his mask, the president hoped to demystify the Subcomandante's aura and make him lose social support. But the incursion had just the opposite effect. In the face of new aggression, more mass protests followed, especially in Mexico City, the place of old Tenochtitlan, where a large crowd assembled wearing ski masks, shouting in solidarity, "We are all Marcos!"

The scene could not be more symbolic. After five hundred years, in the same place where the Aztec Empire had come to an end, people reunited once again to recognize Mexico's historical debt and perhaps feel a little guilt toward those who had been there first.

Conclusion: Mexico

Benito Juárez, universally acclaimed as one of the best, if not the best, president of Mexico, once said, "Why is Mexico, my country, so strange that it is formed, half and half, of an inexhaustible source of tenderness and a deep well of bestiality?" Did Juárez have the Mexican flag in mind when he said this, where a noble eagle and a snake fight to death eternally, the symbol of two opposing forces, one from heaven and another from the earth?

Mexico is a country of contrasts, from its geography to its people. Its history is one of encounter and conflict, of triumphs that become failures once they display their limitations to solve the needs of a society, a society that was born from one of those encounters, a violent one between Montezuma and Hernán Cortés. In 1810, the independence started by fathers Miguel Hidalgo and José María Morelos gave rise to a country that became addicted to solving its problems with coups and proclamations. The ardor of the 19th-century Liberals to create an egalitarian society led them to excesses that provoked an equally bitter reaction, which led to France's intervention and a tragic monarchy. The Mexican Revolution of 1910, which fought for agrarian reform and social justice, ended up being authoritarian and anticlerical, engendering first the Cristero War and then the broad social unrest of the 1960s. Therefore, it is only appropriate to say that today's Mexico, a 200-year-old independent country with ancient roots, is still looking for that long-awaited balance and definitive encounter. "Mexico is a beautiful country, one of the most beautiful on Earth," wrote the intellectual Jesús Silva-Herzog, "but it is still under construction, and what matters most is to finish the job, and the sooner the better."

However, not everything has been violent. From these encounters between races, cultures, and ideas, so often bloody, Mexico has managed to get the best out of its men and women, who have given the world many contributions. Although civilization might be possible without them, no one would want to live in a world without them. The Maya invented the zero around 350 BCE and used it as a placeholder in their complex calendars; also—although other countries would wince at this statement—they invented football (soccer for those American readers) or at least a very similar game. The Aztecs were the first civilization in the world to grant universal and free education, regardless of age, class, or gender in a world where, until recently, school was reserved for the rich and noble. The Aztecs were also the creators of the first zoo in the Americas.

Many delicacies, such as chocolate, tequila, avocado, corn tortillas, and popcorn, were all born in Mexico. The world not only fell in love with chocolate, but other cultures decided to preserve its original name in the Nahuatl language: chocolate in English, *sokoláta* in Greek, *čokoláda* in Czech, *shukulata* in Arabic, and *shukuledi* in Zulu. In the case of tortillas, the basic element of the famous taco, there is evidence that it was prepared in Oaxaca three thousand years ago; when it comes to the avocado, the base of the well-known guacamole, there is evidence that it was consumed ten thousand years ago in the state of Puebla. Not in vain, Mexican cuisine is one of the three cuisines in all the world—along with French and Japanese—that is considered as Intangible Cultural Heritage by UNESCO.

The color television was developed by electrical engineer Guillermo González Camarena when he was 23. The contraceptive pill was synthesized by chemist Luis Ernesto Miramontes Cárdenas. In the field of science, Mario Molina, the winner of the Nobel Prize in 1995, demonstrated the mechanism by which the ozone layer is destroyed and noted the thinning of the layer in Antarctica, creating global awareness of the danger of CFCs.

As the 21st century sets in, new historical challenges open for Mexico: the threat of drug trafficking, the problem of migration with the United States, and addressing its regional and economic inequalities, all problems that remain endemic. But new opportunities will also open up in the next years. Mexico might have a leadership position in Latin America, and in the distant future, it will possibly witness, along with its northern neighbor, the birth of a new third country between Mexico and the United States that futurologists call MexAmerica, for lack of a better name.

Mexicans are widely known as hospitable and affectionate to visitors and strangers. "Mexico has a place for foreigners, it has a strange melody," said artist Chavela Vargas, who, although born in Costa Rica, was a self-proclaimed Mexican. "To say Mexico is to say something sweet, sweet Mexico. Mexico is the divine word, the magic word, the wise word. It is about its sound and color that appears in our minds when we say it. It is a smell." If we add Mexico's enormous biodiversity—the territory is home to almost 70 percent of the world's variety of plants and animals—and archeological treasures to the mixture, it is not surprising that it is today the sixth most visited country in the world. And if traveling around its lands makes it an unforgettable and surprising experience for strangers, no less fascinating is the complex and dramatic history of a nation where one of the first civilizations of the planet surged, a people of astronomers and warriors. A history that includes the meeting between Cortés and Montezuma, where globalization really began. With 130 million people, it is, in every sense, a place so recognizable that one can clearly see it from space, a horn with two peninsulas like stretched hands surrounded, just as in ancient times, by azure waters. Mexicans have a saying for that. "They don't come any better than Mexico." Or in Spanish, "*Como México no hay dos.*"

Bibliography

Escalante, Pablo *et al. Nueva Historia Mínima de México.* Mexico: El Colegio de México, 2004.

Gussinyer i Alfonso, Jordi. *México-Tenochtitlan en una Isla. Introducción al urbanismo de una ciudad precolombina.* Spain: Universitat de Barcelona, 2001.

Katz, Friedrich. *The Secret War in Mexico: Europe, the United States, and the Mexican Revolution.* Chicago: University of Chicago Press, 1984.

Khasnabish, Alex. *Zapatistas: Rebellion from the Grassroots to the Global.* Canada: Fernwood Publishing Ltd, 2010.

León-Portilla, Miguel. *El México Antiguo en la Historia Universal.* Mexico: FOEM, 2015.

León-Portilla, Miguel. *The Broken Spears: The Aztec Account of the Conquest of Mexico.* Boston: Beacon Press, 2006.

Meyer, Jean. *La Cristiada. The Mexican People´s War for Religious Liberty.* New York: SquareOne Publishers, 2013.

Restall, Matthew. *When Montezuma Met Cortes: The True Story of the Meeting that Changed History.* New York: HarperCollins, 2018.

Schulenburg, Mariana. *Guadalupe: Visión y Controversia.* Aguascalientes: Libros de México: 2016.

Vázquez Lozano, Gustavo. *The Aztec Eagles. The History of the Mexican Pilots Who Fought in World War II.* Aguascalientes: Libros de Mexico, 2019.

Here's another book by Captivating History
that you might be interested in

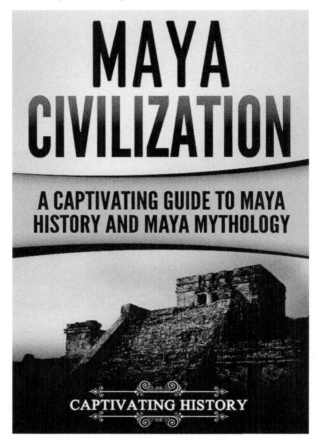